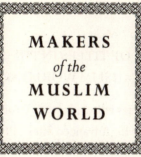

MAKERS
of the
MUSLIM
WORLD

'Abd al-Rahman III

MAKERS
of the
MUSLIM
WORLD

'Abd al-Rahman III
The First Cordoban Caliph

MARIBEL FIERRO

ONEWORLD
ACADEMIC

'ABD AL-RAHMAN III

First published by Oneworld Publications, 2005
Reprinted, 2019, 2020

© Maribel Fierro 2005

ISBN 978-1-85168-384-0
eISBN 978-1-78074-187-1

Typeset by Jayvee, India
Cover and text design by Design Deluxe
Printed and bound in Great Britain by Clays Ltd, Elcograf S.p.A.

Oneworld Publications

10 Bloomsbury Street
London WC1B 3SR

MIX
Paper from
responsible sources
FSC® C018072

CONTENTS

FOREWORD

What is usually referred to as Muslim Spain is consistently rendered al-Andalus in this book (see map on pp. viii–ix). There are two reasons for this. On the one hand, al-Andalus was a political and geographical entity that included territories which belong nowadays to two countries, Spain and Portugal. On the other hand, neither Spain nor Portugal existed as such at the time when al-Andalus did, both countries in fact having been partly formed in the fight against the Muslims of al-Andalus.

Throughout the book, Arabic terms are written without diacritics. The Arabic *'ayn* is represented by '.

Arabic names are composed of a first name, followed by those of the male ancestors. Kinship is expressed through the term *ibn*, meaning "son of" or *bint*, "daughter of", although the latter only appears after the first name, as genealogy is strictly agnatic (descent from a male ancestor through the male line). Examples are Ahmad ibn Muhammad ibn Abi 'Abda or Fatima bint 'Abd Allah ibn Muhammad ibn 'Abd al-Rahman. Another element of the name is the *nisba*, indicating various sorts of affiliation: tribal, geographical, or legal. Examples in corresponding order are al-Lakhmi (from the Arab tribe of Lakhm), al-Qurtubi (from the town of Cordoba), and al-Maliki (belonging to the Maliki school of law). The *kunya* is the part of the name describing a person as the father or mother of somebody, regardless of the existence of a child with that name. Thus 'Abd al-Rahman's *kunya* was Abu l-Mutarrif (father of Mutarrif), but no son of his is known to have been named Mutarrif.

Al-Andalus and North Africa in the Tenth Century

Bay of Biscay

GALICIA

Santiago

ASTURIAS

Oviedo

NAVARRA

León

Pamplona

CASTILLE

Tudela

Huesca

Ebro

Zaragoza

Duero

Medinaceli

Turia

Tajo

Toledo

Valencia

Júcar

Mérida

Guadiana

Lisboa

Badajoz

Denia

Segura

Guadalquivir

Murcia

Madīnat al-Zahrā'

Córdoba

Ecija

Jaén

Sevilla

Carmona

Elvira (Granada)

Bobastro

Pechina

Málaga

Almería

Gibraltar

Algeciras

Orán

ATLANTIC

Tetuán

OCEAN

75 miles
150km

Fez

Map by **MAP***grafix*

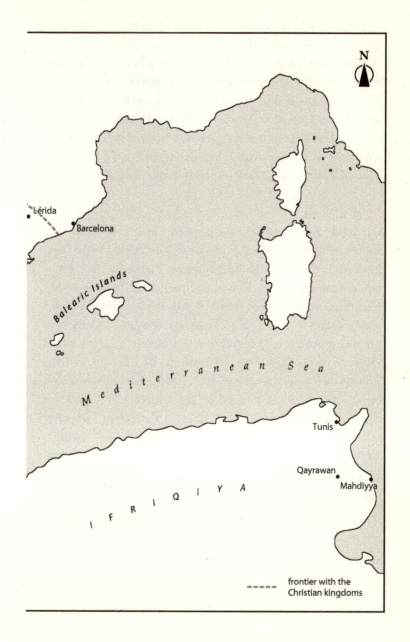

N

Lérida
Barcelona

Balearic Islands

M e d i t e r r a n e a n   S e a

Tunis

Qayrawan
Mahdiyya

I F R I Q I Y A

- - - - - frontier with the
Christian kingdoms

The term "Banu" followed by a name (such as "Banu l-Hajjaj," literally "the sons of al-Hajjaj") indicates an agnatic group.

Dates are given according to the Christian calendar. Sometimes they are rendered as, for example, 948–9: in the Muslim lunar calendar (or hijri calendar, starting in 622, the year of Muhammad's migration from Mecca to Medina), if no specific date is given within a year, the latter may begin in one solar year of the Christian calendar and end in the following. Thus, the hijri year 337 corresponds to the years A.D. 948–9.

I wish to thank Professor Patricia Crone for asking me to write this book, from which I have derived much enjoyment, and for her careful and critical reading. Salvador Peña, Miguel Vega, Michael Lecker, Luis Molina, Manuela Marín and the rest of my colleagues at the Consejo Superior de Investigationes Científicas (CSIC) have contributed to the completion of this work. David Wasserstein's comments and corrections have greatly improved it. Without the help of Pepa Cladera and of the staff of the Biblioteca del Instituto de Filología and the Escuela de Estudios Árabes (CSIC), this book could never have been written. What I heard at the Fourth Conference on Madinat al-Zahra' which took place in Cordoba (November 2003) has undoubtedly influenced my views. Matilde Cerrolaza, Armanda Rodríguez Fierro, Eduardo González-Yarza, Álvaro Alonso, Isabel Colón, Ana Cano Ávila, and most especially David Waines, my father and my son, have aided me in many different ways.

THE FOURTEEN DAYS
OF HAPPINESS OF 'ABD
AL-RAHMAN III (r. 912–61)

'Abd al-Rahman III, the ruler who gave to the Umayyad dynasty in al-Andalus unprecedented strength inside and influence abroad during the first half of the tenth century (he reigned from 912 to 961), was said to have kept a daily written record of his forty-nine years' reign. It revealed, after his death, that he had had only fourteen days of happiness. He did not say which ones they were.

Were those days connected with the most successful campaigns against his foes, on which we have so much information? Was one of them the day he received the oath of allegiance as ruler without meeting any opposition from the rest of his family, in spite of his youth? Or the day he returned victorious to Cordoba after the first military expedition he commanded in person? Or the day when Bobastro, the fortress where his enemies the Hafsunids had managed to resist for years, was conquered? Or the day he proclaimed himself caliph, the title borne by his Umayyad ancestors when they ruled the Islamic world from Damascus? Or the days the rebellious towns of Toledo and Zaragoza were finally overcome? Or the day the magnificent hall he built in Madinat al-Zahra', the town he had founded near Cordoba, was finished? Were those days of happiness connected with his private life, about which we know so little?

Whichever they were, the point of the anecdote is that those days were but few for a man who enjoyed power, authority, wealth, military success, beautiful women, and many children. Were they few because his personality or character precluded him from enjoying life? Were they few because most of his life was spent under the pressure of continuous fighting in order first to maintain the unstable rule he had inherited, then to expand and consolidate it? Or were they few because the responsibility of a ruler, a caliph, was such that happiness, both regarding this life and the other, necessarily became a rarity?

The anecdote, in fact, might just belong to the repertoire of things that are said about rulers and that make the stuff of ancient moral tales and modern soap operas. A hugely successful soap opera that was shown with equal success in Mexico and post-Soviet Russia had the telling title "The rich also cry," and many in their deprivation took comfort from this. An anecdote telling that a caliph only had fourteen days of happiness was intended to teach that happiness is not dependent on the things one owns, but on the way one lives one's life. Consequently, the poor man and the rich man have equal opportunities of achieving happiness.

Such an anecdote could have been told about any other powerful man. The fact that 'Abd al-Rahman III is the protagonist is an indication that he had acquired literary and symbolic dimensions. And this was also helped by the fact that his triumph was closely connected with fall. 'Abd al-Rahman III's pacification of al-Andalus, his consolidation of Umayyad rule, and his relationships with such powerful political and religious figures as the Byzantine emperor, the Fatimid caliph of North Africa, and the German emperor, were all achievements destined to be of short duration. Some fifty years after his death, the caliphate he had established was crumbling, never to recover, and Madinat al-Zahra' was lying in ruins. The fourteen days of happiness might also stand for the brevity of 'Abd al-Rahman III's success.

And yet al-Andalus had been changed by him for ever. Among the changes brought by the first Umayyad caliph in the Islamic west, and developed under his successors, a not unimportant one was the impulse given to the emergence of a distinct identity for al-Andalus.

But what exactly was al-Andalus?

2

AL-ANDALUS BEFORE THE SECOND UMAYYAD CALIPHATE (EIGHTH–NINTH CENTURIES)

WHAT WAS AL-ANDALUS?

Al-Andalus was the name given by Muslims to the Iberian peninsula, and in a more restricted sense, the name given to the territory under Muslim rule. That territory was not always the same.

Until the eleventh century, most of the Iberian peninsula was controlled by Muslims, except for the northern regions, where small Christian kingdoms emerged. That the core of Muslim settlement and rule lay in the south is indicated by the location chosen for the capital of al-Andalus. The Visigoths, the former Germanic rulers of the Iberian peninsula, who had entered from the north, had established their political and religious capital in Toledo, situated roughly in the middle of the peninsula. Toledo fell into Muslim hands when Muslim armies conquered the Iberian peninsula in the second decade of the eighth century and it had a crucial role in frontier politics, being often referred to as the "capital" of the Middle Frontier of al-Andalus. But it was Cordoba, a town further south, that became the seat of the Muslim governors and later of the Umayyad rulers of al-Andalus.

In 1085, Toledo was occupied by Alfonso VI, king of Castille and León, and lost forever to the Muslims. By then, the Umayyad caliphate founded by 'Abd al-Rahman III in the tenth century had collapsed, and al-Andalus was divided into the so-called Party kingdoms, a division that gave the Christians the opportunity to interfere in their internal politics and more importantly, to extract monetary payments from them. The strengthening of their military capabilities as the Christians established "societies organized for war" ran parallel to the inability of the Muslim inhabitants of al-Andalus to raise competent armies to face the Christian enemies from the north. After the fall of Toledo showed how dangerous their situation had become, the Party kings realized the urgency of looking for help.

Help came from the Almoravids, the Berbers who had managed to found for the first time a unified and solid state in what is now Morocco. The military assistance given by the Almoravid emir to the Andalusi rulers was soon transformed into the latter's political submission and eventual elimination. By the end of the eleventh century, al-Andalus thus lost its independence as an autonomous state. Almoravid rule was shaken at the end of the third decade of the twelfth century by attempts by the Andalusis to regain local control of their land. The polities started by members of the urban elites, military men, and charismatic saints who seized power in different parts of al-Andalus were, however, destroyed when al-Andalus once more became a dependency of a powerful Berber empire, this time the Almohad empire that had arisen in the south of Morocco. But the Almohads eventually also proved to be unable to stop the Christian military advance. Cordoba fell in 1236, followed by other important towns such as Murcia in 1243 and Seville in 1248.

Christian conquest obliged many Muslims to migrate to Muslim lands across the Straits of Gibraltar, while others stayed, living as a religious minority under Christian rule. Some settled in the only remaining Muslim state, Granada, where an Andalusi military and charismatic leader had succeeded in creating a small state. It survived for almost three centuries (from the mid-thirteenth century to 1492) under the so-called Nasrid dynasty by taking advantage of its enemies' weaknesses and by making itself useful to them at the same time. The survival of Nasrid Granada had its roots in its adaptability to changing circumstances and in its inherent fragility, reflected so well in the cheap materials used to build the Alhambra, the beautiful palace that has kept alive until today the memory of the last Muslim kingdom in the Iberian peninsula.

During the eight centuries of its existence as an Islamic society, the Muslims who inhabited al-Andalus kept close links with the rest of the Islamic religious community to which they belonged. The religious duty of performing the pilgrimage to Mecca and travelling in order to study with teachers abroad were powerful means through which the Andalusi elites sustained, while transforming and re-interpreting, their own Muslim identity and that of the population they took care of and led as scholars, prayer-leaders, judges, jurists, secretaries, literati, poets, and saints. Along with the feeling of belonging to a universal religious community, they had a distinct, but not static, Andalusi identity that separated them from other Muslims. It was an identity that could embrace the different ethnic backgrounds of those who inhabited the Iberian peninsula under Muslim rule and that could also embrace members of the other two religious communities, Jews and Christians, who were under that same rule. This Andalusi identity is generally considered to have been promoted especially by the Cordoban Umayyad caliphs, beginning with 'Abd al-Rahman III, as it helped them strengthen their rule. And this had to do with the way al-Andalus had been conquered and by whom, and with the way the Umayyads, dethroned in the east by the 'Abbasids, established their rule over its Muslim population.

ARABS AND BERBERS, THE MUSLIM TRIBESMEN WHO CONQUERED AL-ANDALUS

Muslim troops first crossed the Straits of Gibraltar in 711, and in a few years the former Visigothic kingdom, weakened by internal dissension, was destroyed. Those troops were dependent on the Muslim military command in North Africa and, through it, on the Umayyad caliph who then ruled the Islamic empire from his seat in Damascus. Ethnically, the members of those troops were Arabs and Berbers.

The number of Arabs among the first Muslim conquerors was small compared with that of Berbers, but they enjoyed a privileged status as Arabs. The link between being Muslim and being Arab was at the time still very powerful. The Arabs had been the first converts to Islam, a religion revealed in the seventh century to an Arab prophet and contained in a sacred book written in Arabic. Until the mid-eighth century, conversion to Islam by those who were not Arabs entailed adoption of the status of client (*mawla*, pl. *mawali*) of an Arab tribesman or of another convert already endowed with a patron. Freed slaves likewise became clients of their former masters. Islamicization, the adoption of the new religion and of the new social and political norms and patterns upheld by it, went hand in hand with Arabicization, involving a new sacred language and often, in the long run, loss of the mother tongue.

The Arab element among the Muslim conquerors of al-Andalus increased after 739, the year when a Berber rebellion broke out in North Africa. The Umayyad caliph in Damascus sent a powerful army to put an end to it, but the resistance of the Berbers was strong. The Syrian troops were defeated in 741. With what was left of the army, the commander Balj ibn Bishr al-Qushayri took refuge in Ceuta, a town separated from the Iberian peninsula by a short distance across the sea. The military governor of al-Andalus sent ships so that the Syrians could cross the Straits of Gibraltar. In exchange, Balj helped the governor fight those Berbers who had followed the rebellion of their North African tribesmen and were causing trouble to the Arabs in the Iberian peninsula. But cooperation between the two Arab commanders did not last long. Balj eventually got rid of the military governor and took his place. Arabic sources refer to Balj's troops as the "second wave" of Muslim conquerors who settled in the Iberian peninsula.

Much information is given in the sources about the tribal alignments of the Arabs who conquered the Iberian peninsula and settled there. The main division was that between Northern (Qays) and Southern (Yemen) Arabs, a division that was imported to al-Andalus from the east. How we should understand the fights between Qays and Yemen in the history of the first two centuries of the Islamic world has been a hotly debated issue. Were they real tribal fights showing that tribalism could not only survive but be an integral part of the new socio-political order? Did they indicate deep political and social divisions, so that tribes were actually acting as political parties in that new order? Or were they the language through which factions of the conquerors gave expression to the allegiances of their constituencies? The latter seems to have been the case, both in the east and in al-Andalus. Here, the memory of battles fought elsewhere and of old grievances bitterly resented served as fuel to warm up old divisions and to cook new ones among the conquering elite.

The tribal and military structure of the Arab population of al-Andalus was functional for some time. The organization of the army was somewhat different from elsewhere. For the most part, Arab-Muslim armies were settled in newly established garrison towns, such as Kufa in Iraq, Old Cairo in Egypt, and Qayrawan in North Africa, where the Muslim minority could preserve its identity and military organization, and where the distribution of the soldiers' pay took place. No such garrison towns were founded in al-Andalus.

The patterns of military settlement followed in al-Andalus had important consequences for the relationships between the conquerors and the conquered and also for the imposition of a central authority. The first wave of Arabs and Berbers who conquered the Iberian peninsula, called in the sources the *baladiyyun*, settled all over the land and became landowners. They appropriated lands without regard for the fifth to which the state was legally entitled, an issue which caused embarrassment in later times. Under the governor al-Samh ibn Malik, an attempt was made to secure for the Muslim state a fifth of the conquered lands, but apparently with limited success. In any case, fiscal control was extended and systematized in al-Andalus during the years of al-Samh's governorship (719–21) and those of his successors.

The different regiments (*jund*s) that made up Balj's Syrian army (and which were named according to their geographical provenance) were settled on the land, without being granted ownership of it, according to an arrangement devised in 743. The *jund*s were assigned to specific districts: the *jund* of

Damascus was settled at Granada (this region was known at the time as Elvira), the *jund* of Hims at Seville and Niebla, the *jund* of Jordan at Málaga, the *jund* of Qinnasrin at Jaén, the *jund* of Palestine at Algeciras and Sidonia, and the *jund* of Egypt at Beja and Tudmir. The *jund*s received a third of the taxes paid by Christians in the districts in question. They were probably put in charge of collecting them, too, thus obtaining fiscal control over the territories to which they were assigned and becoming involved in their administration. After appropriating a third of the payments made by Christians, the *jund*s were in principle obliged to turn over the rest to the central government. They were also obliged to pay tax to the governor or representative of the Umayyad administrative apparatus on income they retained for their upkeep. However, the hold of the central government over the Muslim population of al-Andalus decreased after the governorship of Abu l-Khattar, while the influence and power of the Syrian regiments increased. When the first Umayyad emir, 'Abd al-Rahman ibn Mu'awiya, rose to power in al-Andalus, his policy was directed, as we shall see, at countering the political dominance acquired by the *jund*s.

The conquerors of the first wave, those who came in 711 and shortly afterwards, were mainly Berbers, the indigenous population of North Africa, a region recently incorporated into the Islamic empire, so they were recent converts to the new religion.

Most of them settled in tribal groups in rural areas, especially along the emerging frontier of al-Andalus, leading a mostly autonomous life difficult to recover from obscurity, although archaeological research is now illuminating certain aspects of it (for example, certain patterns of irrigation might reflect Berber tribal organization). Their existence is revealed in the written sources when they became involved in armed conflict with the Cordoban ruler or his representatives. Sometimes, this armed conflict assumed a religious form, characterized by leadership of a charismatic figure associated with messianic expectations. The military resources provided by Berber tribal organization allowed some of their leaders to become rulers of Party kingdoms in the eleventh century, after the collapse of the Umayyad caliphate. The sources are almost completely silent regarding the survival of Berber languages.

Unlike the Berbers who settled in rural areas, those who lived in urban settlements, having entered the state administration or become scholars, reached a higher degree of Arabicization and Islamicization. Most of them appear as clients of the Umayyads. As 'Abd al-Rahman III was keen to remind his Berber allies, the conversion to Islam of the Berber population of North Africa had taken place when the Islamic world was being ruled by his ancestors, the Umayyad caliphs of Damascus, thus implying that the Berbers as a people were clients of the Umayyad family.

THE CONQUERED POPULATION AND THE PROCESS OF CONVERSION

When al-Andalus was conquered, the Hispano-Roman population of the Iberian peninsula had been ruled for two centuries by the Visigoths. That population was Christian. There was also a small Jewish community whose existence under Visigothic rule had often been under threat; it was therefore said to have welcomed the new rulers. The legal regulations of the new Muslim rulers involved discrimination against the members of the other two monotheistic faiths, but not persecution, and so the Jewish community was able to live in peace and to thrive. Jews and Christians became *dhimmi*s, or protected groups, in the new political order. Being the "people of the book" who had preceded the Muslim community, they were not forced to convert to the new religion. They could maintain their religious authorities, perform their cult, and solve their conflicts under their own legal ordinances, unless those activities were considered to interfere with the rights of the ruling religious community. Jews and Christians had their survival legally ensured under a discriminatory tolerance. But protection of the law was not a guarantee for long-lasting survival. They were always threatened by conversion and occasionally by persecution.

By the eleventh century al-Andalus was overwhelmingly Muslim, and by the end of the twelfth century there were no noticeable surviving Christian communities. The tenth century is generally considered to have been the period when the balance between a ruling Muslim minority and a Christian majority started to shift to a Muslim majority. The pull towards the rulers' religion and culture, the adoption of which gave or enhanced social status and prestige and which could involve a reduction of taxation, went together with the push represented by the local church's inability to cater effectively for the religious needs of the Christian population.

In al-Andalus, as elsewhere in the early Islamic post-conquest period, the Muslim ruling elite did nothing to favor the conversion of the *dhimmi*s, because of the financial losses it would have meant for them. The Muslim Arabs were military elites who depended for their privileged livelihood on the existence of a mass who, as neither Muslim nor Arab, were not entitled to the same privileges. The reluctance to increase the number of converts must have been especially felt by the Syrians whose upkeep depended on the taxes paid by the Christian rural population. But conversion could not be discouraged in the long run, especially after the Umayyads rose to power and realized how they could derive advantages from it.

Though conversion was not favored at the beginning, the number of Muslims is likely to have increased by other means, and especially by intermarriage. Muslim men could have a maximum of four legal wives and as many concubines as they could afford. Children born to Arab tribesmen and local women or slave concubines were Arab Muslims, regardless of the social status, ethnicity, or religion of the wife. Memory of descent from the conquered population is so exceptional that the single recorded case is worthy of recall.

A noble Visigothic woman called Sarah, her name rendered in Arabic as Sarah al-Qutiyya (Sarah the Goth), was the daughter of Count Ardobast, an extremely rich landowner who became a close collaborator with the Muslim conquerors, collecting taxes from the Christians and suggesting to the governor Abu l-Khattar the pattern of settlement of the Syrian *junds*, which may have preserved a Visigothic custom. Ardobast's lands were eventually confiscated by the first Umayyad emir. His daughter Sarah was married twice to members of the Arab army, and the descendants of these marriages became powerful lineages (such as the Banu l-Hajjaj) in the regions of Seville and Cordoba. Only one branch of those lineages was known as the Banu l-Qutiyya, thus preserving the memory of their grandmother. A member of this branch was the historian Ibn al-Qutiyya, whose history of al-Andalus, written in the tenth century, has been interpreted by some as representing the point of view and the interests of the Andalusi convert population. The fact that his name preserved the memory of his Christian Visigothic ancestor was probably due to the fact that they were descendants of Sarah's first husband, an Umayyad client: they took pride in their maternal ancestry because it was nobler than the paternal line. The descendants of Sarah's second husband, an Arab member of the Syrian army, did not call themselves after their female ancestor: being descendants of an Arab, not of a client, was enough.

According to Islamic law, a Muslim man could marry a Christian or Jewish woman without the latter being obliged to renounce her religion, but no Muslim woman could marry outside her religious community. Children born from non-Muslim women, both males and females, were Muslim. Writing in the tenth century, the eastern traveller and geographer Ibn Hawqal records that in Muslim Sicily there was a region where female children born to Muslim men married to Christian women were allowed to follow their mother's religion, whereas the males became Muslims. This departure from the regulations of Islamic law may have occurred, at least temporarily, in other regions of the early Islamic world, as it seems to reflect a transitional adaptation to the new religious and legal order.

In ninth-century al-Andalus, a similar custom may be behind the behavior of women who were among the so-called Cordoban martyrs. These were Christians in and around Cordoba who sought voluntary martyrdom by publicly insulting the Prophet Muhammad and his religion. The martyrs did not find much support in the Church hierarchy and the movement, which lasted from 850 to 859, with some later isolated episodes, eventually died out. There were many women among these martyrs, and some of them are presented as daughters of Muslim fathers and non-Muslim mothers and as having been educated as Christians. Their status, according to Muslim law, was that of apostates: they were Muslim by birth and therefore could not behave as Christians. But we might have here the result of a practice, similar to that recorded by Ibn Hawqal in Sicily, that came to light at the moment when it was being suppressed. In Andalusi society, by the middle of the ninth century, both the Muslim and non-Muslim populations were becoming increasingly Islamicized, in the sense of having to abide by those standards that were being fixed in normative legal texts and whose implementation was being more strictly monitored by an expanding judicial system.

The search for martyrdom represents a reaction to the tensions created within the Christian community by the process of cultural Arabicization and religious conversion to Islam. Christians living in al-Andalus are often referred to in the secondary literature as "Mozarabs" (meaning "arabicized"), although no Arabic source uses this term. It appears in late Christian sources as a term for Christians who emigrated from al-Andalus to the north of the Iberian peninsula and whose main distinguishing feature in the Christian societies in which they settled was precisely the fact they spoke Arabic and that culturally they resembled Arabs. To apply the term Mozarab indiscriminately to all the Christians who lived in al-Andalus during the eighth–tenth centuries is to assume that they shared a cultural and linguistic identity that many of them did not actually have. In the early period, only those who lived in urban settings with a sizeable Arab population, such as Cordoba, were prone to becoming Arabicized and to being attracted to the ruling elite culture.

The vast majority of the Christian population, however, lived in rural areas and with limited contact with the Arab conquerors and settlers. Even as late as the tenth century, Ibn Hawqal recorded that

> in al-Andalus there is more than one agricultural property on which dwell thousands of people who know nothing of urban life and who are Hispano-Romans professing the Christian religion. There are periods in which they rebel and some of them take refuge in fortresses. They put up a stiff fight, for they are fierce and stubborn. When they cast off the yoke of obedience, it is hard to make them return to it, unless they are exterminated, and that is a difficult, prolonged process.

In this text, nothing is said about the language spoken by these rural Christians, but it must have been the Romance language, deriving from Latin. It is only around the middle or the end of the eleventh century that the local population of al-Andalus seems to have become largely monolingual, speaking almost exclusively Arabic and leaving behind a phase of Romance/Arabic bilingualism. By the twelfth century only Arabic was spoken, a process that coincided with the disappearance of the Christian community through conversion, expulsion, or emigration.

Linguistic Arabicization was especially deep among the Jews of al-Andalus. Paradoxically this process went together with the survival and flourishing of Hebrew as their religious and cultural language, whereas the Christians, responding to spoken linguistic change, had started by the tenth century a process of Arabicization of their sacred literature, as shown for example by the Arabic translation of the Psalms and of the Church canons.

Ibn Hawqal's text records the military capabilities that Christians living under Muslim rule still had at the beginning of the tenth century, before those capabilities were destroyed by 'Abd al-Rahman III through his defeat of the Hafsunids, the *muwallad* rebels who had found much support among those rural Christian communities. The term *muwallad* has been used by modern historians of al-Andalus to refer to the descendants of Christians who had converted to Islam, although the proper meaning of the term is "anyone who, without being of Arab origin, is born among the Arabs and has been raised as an Arab", in other words, someone who has become linguistically and culturally Arabicized, with no indication of his religion. But because being an Arab in al-Andalus implied being a Muslim, it could be assumed that those who had been Arabicized converted, sooner or later, to the Arabs' religion. In any case,

the term *muwalladun* (here rendered as Muwallads) is used
by the Andalusi Arabic sources to refer to the indigenous
population of converts, if only when they were involved in
armed conflicts with the Umayyad rulers and with the Arab and
Berber lords who controlled certain areas of the Iberian peninsula during the ninth century. The reason they engaged in
armed conflict as converts is related to the impact that the
arrival of an Umayyad immigrant had on the tribal polities of
the Iberian peninsula.

THE UMAYYAD EMIRS: CENTRALIZATION, LAW, AND CLIENTAGE

In A.D. 750 the Umayyad caliphate of Damascus fell, and a new
dynasty, the 'Abbasids, became the rulers of the Islamic
empire. They moved their capital to Iraq, where they built
Baghdad. The new caliphs presented themselves as having a
better claim to rule than the Umayyads. Whereas the latter
could only claim to belong to the Prophet's tribe, the Quraysh,
and to the family of the third caliph, 'Uthman, the 'Abbasids
were the descendants of a close relative of the Prophet
Muhammad, his paternal uncle, al-'Abbas. By stressing their
kinship with the Apostle of God, the 'Abbasids were also down-
playing Arab ancestry as the key element for deciding who were
the legitimate rulers of the Muslim community. In that, they
were following the path taken by the Shi'is, for whom only a
member of the close family of the Prophet – a closeness which
was variably interpreted – could become the "vicar of God"
or caliph, and legitimately rule the Islamic community. This
was an important move on the part of the 'Abbasids. A crucial
element of 'Abbasid policy was precisely the promotion of a
Muslim identity superseding the different ethnic backgrounds

and thus putting an end to the Arab supremacy that had characterized the Umayyad period. Somewhat paradoxically, this
went together with the promotion – and also invention – of
Arabic culture as a means to counteract non-Arab, especially
Persian, claims to cultural superiority.

The 'Abbasids' seizure of power was accompanied by a
bloody massacre of the Umayyad family. Very few survived.
One of them was 'Abd al-Rahman ibn Mu'awiya. The story of
how he managed to escape 'Abbasid persecution would make
an exciting script for a Hollywood movie. Together with his
loyal client, the manumitted slave Badr, he fled from Syria to
North Africa. He was located by 'Abbasid agents in one of his
refuges among Umayyad Berber clients and had to flee again.
His mother was a Berber woman, and 'Abd al-Rahman ibn
Mu'awiya sought refuge among her tribe, the Nafza, but fear-
ing for his life he had to move again, coming closer to the
Iberian peninsula. During this period, he made contact with
Umayyad clients settled in al-Andalus.

Al-Andalus was then immersed in internecine fights among
competing factions of the tribal army, expressed through the
division Northern (Qaysi)/Southern (Yemeni) Arabs. The
leader of the former was al-Sumayl, a strong and clever man
who managed to have his men appointed as governors of
al-Andalus. In the battle of Secunda in the year 747, al-Sumayl
had the upper hand over the Yemeni faction. But that did not
bring lasting peace. Al-Sumayl was approached by Umayyad
clients who wanted him to help them get 'Abd al-Rahman ibn
Mu'awiya to the Iberian peninsula. But al-Sumayl knew that
the arrival of the Umayyad would endanger the independence
of the tribal groups, a possibility that he expressed in saying that
'Abd al-Rahman belonged to a clan of such importance that if
any of its members urinated in the Iberian peninsula, all its
tribal leaders would be drowned. So he refused to help.

The Umayyad clients, unable to secure the support of the Northern Arab faction (to which the Umayyads belonged), turned to the Yemenis. 'Abd al-Rahman crossed the Straits of Gibraltar in the year 755, and one year later his rule over al-Andalus started, lasting until the year 788. He and his successors had to fight hard to consolidate their reign in Cordoba and to have it acknowledged by the Muslim population of al-Andalus. 'Abd al-Rahman I had also to start securing revenues and properties for himself and his family and clients, thus raising again the issue of the fifth and alienating the *baladiyyun*, who had become landowners after the conquest. He confiscated the lands of Count Ardobast and put an end to the autonomy that the region of Murcia had enjoyed since the treaty negotiated by its ruler Tudmir at the time of the conquest.

As the Arab *jund*s were in charge of collecting taxes, the governors did not always receive the revenues allotted to the central government. The first Umayyad ruler of al-Andalus tried to seize control by weakening the *jund*s, playing one faction against another, and by recruiting Berber and slave contingents who owed allegiance to him personally. He also invited members of his clan to settle in al-Andalus in order to extend his support group. The *jund* system was maintained, but with certain changes. A system of stipends was introduced in the Umayyad period, according to which the Arab troops received payment for campaigns they had conducted. Receipt of such payments was regulated by a rigid hierarchy controlled by the sovereign. The absence of regular wages is explained by the existence of grants, whether in the form of lands or taxes, which guaranteed their upkeep.

The Umayyad emirs had often to fight hard against those who contested their rule, resorting in some cases to brutal repression. Especially troublesome was the frontier, not to be understood as a modern border between countries, but as the entire territory alongside the enemy's lands which was open to incursions and campaigns.

In these frontier regions local lineages ruled while paying only nominal obeisance to the Umayyads. Toledo rebelled many times. Its resistance to outside control was never expressed through the establishment of a dynasty-like lineage similar to those emerging in the Upper March, the Banu Qasi, and in the Lower March, the Banu al-Jilliqi, both of native origin. These lineages and the Umayyads played a complex game in which periods of submission alternated with periods of autonomy sometimes brought to an end through brutal repression. The leaders of Toledo were massacred in 797 during the reign of al-Hakam I (r. 796–822). The capital itself tasted al-Hakam I's repressive policies.

In A.D. 817, al-Hakam I had to face the revolt of the *rabad* in Cordoba. The *rabad* was a quarter situated on the edge of the Guadalquivir river, just opposite the palace and the Friday mosque. Its population was formed by artisans, but also by members of the emerging group of religious scholars and jurists, many of whom had family connections with the army and with the market. The revolt was based on dissatisfaction with the fiscal practices of the Umayyad emir, who had imposed more control and higher taxes, and also with his growing reliance on slave soldiers and his own family and relatives. The emir was in real danger of being killed during the revolt, but with the help of the slave soldiers, relatives, and clients that the population resented, he eventually managed to gain the upper hand. The repression of the rebels was ferocious: many were killed together with their women and children, and of those who survived, many were expelled from the town. From then onwards, the Umayyads could count on the frightened loyalty of the inhabitants of their capital.

A shift from the policy of repression to that of conviction took place under the reign of al-Hakam I's successor, 'Abd al-Rahman II (822–52). An alliance was then established between the Umayyad emir and the growing body of religious scholars: the former consulted the latter and the latter paid obeisance to the former while counselling the rest of the population to do the same. It has been debated to what extent scholars emerged in al-Andalus with or without the support of the Umayyad rulers. However this may be, it is a fact that a legal school such as that of the Iraqi scholar Abu Hanifa (d. 767), which was enormously influential elsewhere at the time, did not succeed in the Iberian peninsula because it was associated with Shi'i leanings and with the 'Abbasids, and was therefore unacceptable to the Umayyads. The legal trend associated with Medina, and most specifically with its famous jurist Malik ibn Anas, became predominant in al-Andalus, and very soon functioned as the backbone of an emerging Andalusi identity.

Biographies of the judges reflect the changes taking place in the Muslim population. Judges had at first been in charge of Muslims who were soldiers and Arabs, and had therefore been Arabs and members of the army themselves. But from the reign of 'Abd al-Rahman II onwards, judges had to deal with an increasing non-Arab population and also to abide by a legal doctrine that in principle did not take into account differences between Arabs and non-Arabs or old and new Muslims. In order to ensure that this legal doctrine was followed by judges, a consultative body of religious scholars was attached to the court. Those scholars were non-Arabs long before a non-Arab was appointed as judge.

Umayyad policy led to a weakening of the power of the Syrian *junds* and, at the same time, promoted conversion to Islam by offering converts opportunities for social and economic advancement. From the times of the Umayyad emir

Muhammad (r. 852–86) onwards, converts could be found in positions of prestige and authority, and non-Arabs began to be appointed as judges.

At the same time, the tolerance of Christian officials diminished. The Christian secretary Qumis ibn Antunyan was active during the emirate of Muhammad. Notables of Arab origin and members of Umayyad client families resented the growing influence of a Christian in the bureaucratic apparatus. Because of their pressure, Qumis converted in order to keep his position. He was a contemporary of the so-called Cordoban martyrs, whose Christian resistance movement, as we have seen, was a reaction against the increasing Islamicization of the society in which they lived.

Malikism spread in al-Andalus during the ninth century and became its official doctrine in the tenth century. Under Malikism, free non-Arabs who converted to Islam were regarded as clients of the Muslim community as a whole, and not of the individual or group with whom they had renounced their former religion. Those converts therefore did not acquire Arabic tribal affiliations in their names, and this must have been considered quite appropriate by the Umayyads and their ruling elites, as converts' loyalty could be shifted from the Arab tribes to the Umayyad emirs, representatives of the religious community at large. The new Muslims and their descendants had no special legal status among the Malikis, unless they were freedmen, although this does not mean that "new Muslims" or converts could not in practice suffer political, social, and economic discrimination compared with "old Muslims."

If the Umayyads were happy with the new legal doctrine regarding the suppression of the individual tie of clientage upon conversion, as it helped them become substitutive universal patrons, some of those who had converted under the old system were also happy with the new ways. This is illustrated by the case of the Banu Qasi.

This family, who played a crucial political and military role in the Upper Frontier during the Umayyad period, had as its ancestor one Casius, described by the eleventh-century scholar and genealogist Ibn Hazm as a "count of the frontier in the times of the Visigoths." This Casius was said to have traveled to Damascus where he converted to Islam under the Umayyad caliph al-Walid (r. 705–15), and according to the legal regulations of the time, he became his client and boasted of this relationship. There was, however, another story about his patron upon conversion, namely that he was a man called Hassan ibn Yasar al-Hudhali, who was the judge of Zaragoza at the time of 'Abd al-Rahman I's arrival in the Iberian peninsula in the year 756. When this version reached Muhammad ibn Lubb (d. 898), a member of the Banu Qasi family, he sought Hassan's son and killed him for having put the tale into circulation.

Why this reaction? Muhammad ibn Lubb's career shows that his rivalry with other members of the Banu Qasi led him to seek the Umayyad emir's support, and he remained loyal to the ruler for a long period of time. In addition, Umayyad elites were generally considered to be Umayyad clients, as we shall see, so Muhammad ibn Lubb must have had a vested interest in promoting the version according to which his ancestor had converted at the hands of an Umayyad caliph. A version that attached him to an Arab tribe would have been all the more repugnant to him in that his most serious opponent for the control of Zaragoza was an Arab, Muhammad ibn 'Abd al-Rahman al-Tujibi, whose family had received the support of the Umayyads in order to weaken the Banu Qasi's power. This episode could also be taken to suggest that Hassan's family, the alleged patrons by conversion of the Banu Qasi, may have also claimed certain rights arising upon such conversion.

EXTERNAL ENEMIES

Al-Andalus is often described in Muslim sources as an island, surrounded on three sides by the sea and by Christians on the other. And these Christians could be dangerous.

The Christians of the Carolingian empire, although exposed to raids by the Muslims of al-Andalus by both land and sea, were able to stop Muslim advance north and south of the Pyrenees. Their own attempts at military expansion inside Muslim territory failed, except for the conquest of Barcelona in 801, but even so they influenced the Christian kingdoms established in the northern regions of the Iberian peninsula both politically and religiously. By the end of the ninth century, however, the kings of Asturias/León developed a new claim: that they ruled as descendants and inheritors of the Visigoths, and therefore had a right to all the lands once ruled by them. They became a real threat to the Muslims, slowly extending their influence over the Duero valley and leading military attacks against them in the reigns of Ordoño I (r. 850–66) and Alfonso III (r. 866–910).

South of the Pyrenees, the tribal aristocracy of the area of Navarra had managed to establish a monarchy in the first half of the ninth century. The Arista dynasty had close political and kinship links with the Muwallad Banu Qasi and 'Abd al-Rahman III's grandmother was said to be the daughter of one of the Arista rulers, Fortún Garcés or Íñiguez (r. 870–905). In the year 905, Sancho Garcés, of the Jimena family, dethroned Fortún Íñiguez and was proclaimed king. His wife was Toda, a member of the Arista family, and therefore she had kinship ties with 'Abd al-Rahman III. The lives of both will cross a few times. The new dynasty established alliances with the kingdom of León, as the Banu Qasi's influence greatly diminished, and also with the county of Castille. The Jimena kings succeded in expanding their territories towards the Ebro valley.

If the Christians were a danger by land, the Vikings were a danger by sea. In 844, they attacked Lisbon and Seville, sailing up the Guadalquivir river. These attacks show the naval weakness of the Umayyads at the time and in fact it was the Viking danger that moved the Umayyad emirs to build a navy that could defend the coasts of al-Andalus. When new Viking attacks took place in 858 and 861, Umayyad ships were now guarding the coasts. But during the Umayyad emirate, the maritime regions of al-Andalus were mostly inert, something that would change under 'Abd al-Rahman III.

Piracy by Berber and local sailors is recorded in the Mediterranean area. The pirates' target was the capture of slaves, a flourishing trade for centuries in the Mediterranean. Between 888 and 894, these pirates managed to establish a permanent settlement in Fraxinetum (La Garde Freinet, in the south of France) that would last until the year 975. During the same period, Andalusi sailors settled in Tenes and Oran, two ports in the North African coast that played an important role in Mediterranean trade during the tenth century.

Non-Muslims living or moving along land or maritime frontiers were not the only enemies of the Umayyads. The 'Abbasids had made unsuccessful attempts at recovering al-Andalus, and some tribal leaders had tried to win their support in order to legitimize their bid for power. But the Aghlabids in Ifriqiya (Tunis), who were in theory representatives of the 'Abbasids, were in practice independent rulers, who never engaged in military confrontation with the Umayyads, although they gave their support to Andalusi rebels such as Ibn Hafsun. On the contrary, there was an intense commercial and cultural exchange between al-Andalus and Ifriqiya, and most ninth-century Andalusi scholars studied in Qayrawan with Maliki teachers.

In what is now Morocco, a member of the family of the Prophet, Idris ibn 'Abd Allah, had founded a dynasty at roughly the same time as 'Abd al-Rahman I. Like the latter, Idris I had to escape from the east, in his case after a failed attempt by his brother, Muhammad al-Nafs al-Zakiyya, to seize power as the Mahdi, a messianic figure. Having escaped many dangers during his passage through North Africa, Idris finally reached the Maghreb (modern Morocco). 'Abd al-Rahman I had found support among the Umayyad clients and the Arabs, but there were no Arab settlements in the area where Idris took refuge. His supporters were Berbers. As an Umayyad, 'Abd al-Rahman I claimed the right to rule as a descendant of 'Uthman, the third caliph who, like the caliphs before and after him, was a member of the Arab tribe of Quraysh. Idris, on the other hand, was not just a Qurashi, but a member of the Prophet's inner family, a descendant of 'Ali, the cousin of the Prophet who married the latter's daughter Fatima, through their son al-Hasan. He thus qualified as a legitimate leader (imam) of the Muslim community, according to the Shi'is. Idris and his descendants were Shi'is only in the sense that their political claim was based on their ancestry, as shown by the coins they minted. However, those coins also show that some Idrisids claimed to be the Mahdi, indicating that they were not alien to the idea that as imams they had a special religious status. Urban life in Morocco was extremely restricted compared to al-Andalus, and no body of scholars seems to have been formed around the Idrisids. Since it was usually scholars who wrote the sources on which we depend, we do not know much about Idrisid doctrine, if there was such a thing. The Idrisids soon became culturally Berberized and politically fragmented, posing no real threat to the Umayyads. Another Shi'i dynasty was however destined to have a decisive influence in the destiny of al-Andalus.

The Fatimids were Isma'ili Shi'is, believing that legitimate rule was limited to the descendants of Husayn, the other son of Fatima and 'Ali, and that among them the imams, the inheritors of the Prophet as religious and political leaders, were those who descended from Isma'il, who had predeceased his father Ja'far al-Sadiq (d. 765). The imam inherited the charismatic powers of the Prophet, could perform miracles, was infallible, and possessed supernatural knowledge.

In A.D. 909, the Fatimids became the rulers of an area that corresponds to present-day Tunis and parts of Libya and Algeria. Like the Umayyads and the Idrisids, they came from the east to North Africa. Isma'ili propagandists had previously extended their doctrine among the Berber Kutama, who provided military power. With this Berber support, the Fatimids defeated the Sunni rulers of Ifriqiya, the Aghlabids. The Fatimids established a Shi'i caliphate rival to that of the 'Abbasids, proclaiming their right to rule as vicars of God on earth. It was mostly as a reaction against the threat posed by the Fatimid caliph that 'Abd al-Rahman III would proclaim himself caliph, the rightful heir of the former Umayyad caliphs in Damascus. But before he claimed the caliphal title, he had to regain control of a land where Umayyad rule had been greatly weakening for some years.

3

THE COLLAPSE OF UMAYYAD POWER AND ITS RECOVERY BY 'ABD AL-RAHMAN III (912–28)

I shall speak about the battle-days of the best of men; one who
    has been adorned with generosity and courage;
One who has destroyed unbelief and rebellion and sundered
    sedition and schism.
For we were experiencing a moment of darkness intense as
    the night, as well as a civil war; being like the scum and
    rubbish [swept] by the torrent,
Until that worshipper of the Clement who is the most eminent
    of the Banu Marwan was invested with power.
Being supported [by God] he appointed a sword from the
    edges of which death flowed, to judge over his enemies.
While he saluted royal power at dawn along with the
    new moon, so that they both arose in the morning like
    two rivals in beauty.

Ibn 'Abd Rabbihi (transl. J.T. Monroe)

MUSLIMS AGAINST MUSLIMS: THE UMAYYAD CONFRONTATION WITH ARABS, BERBERS, AND MUWALLADS

The Umayyad 'Abd al-Rahman II (r. 822–52) had promoted in al-Andalus the 'Abbasid way of doing things. This policy had its mundane aspect in court life, which was thoroughly transformed by the Iraqi musician Ziryab, who entered al-Andalus in 822 and under the patronage of the Umayyad emir introduced many innovations in music, food, clothing, hair styles, and etiquette. The royal production of official robes and textiles (*tiraz*) was established. At the same time, a scholarly class of jurists and scholars started to emerge in the Umayyad capital, Cordoba, and in other towns. The degree to which a growing central administration penetrated the different districts of al-Andalus is seen in the increasing information offered by the sources about the emir's nomination of military commanders, governors, tax collectors, and judges. Centralizing policies were continued by the Umayyad emirs Muhammad (r. 852–86) and al-Mundhir (r. 886–8).

As the Umayyads struggled to consolidate and expand their grip on al-Andalus, opposition to them, described by the sources as rebellion, exploded from time to time. The tensions between local elites and central government were endemic in the frontier regions. There, the Umayyads often limited themselves to acknowledging the existing autonomy of local rulers by granting them official nomination in exchange for recognition and the payment of taxes. In other regions of al-Andalus, local Arab and Berber groups also defied Umayyad officials and their policies. A new situation arose when Muwallads or leaders belonging to the local population appeared. As indicated in the previous chapter, *muwallad* means "anyone who, without being of Arab origin, is born among the Arabs and has been raised as an Arab." This linguistic and cultural Arabization of the local population usually, but not necessarily, went hand in hand with conversion to Islam.

The second half of the ninth century is a period known as the *fitna*, an Arabic term for civil strife and political and religious dissent. The Umayyads saw their grip on al-Andalus loosening, while Arabs, Berbers, and Muwallads asserted their leadership in towns and fortresses, sometimes fighting each other, sometimes establishing alliances with other rebels, sometimes acknowledging Umayyad sovereignty before rebelling again. Because 'Abd al-Rahman III eventually managed to put an end to this period of constant warfare, the ninth century is understood as a period of transition between the conquest society and the final triumph of an Islamic society as represented by the new Umayyad caliphate.

The transition took the form of a long contest in which the Umayyads had to face, on the one hand, the factional and tribal groupings into which the bulk of the conquering population (Arabs and Berbers) was divided, and, on the other hand, the Muwallads. Historians have different views on how to understand the latter's political behavior. For some, the Muwallad leaders were descendants of the Visigothic lords, who had managed to maintain their feudal rule over specific territories and lived on rents from the peasants. This means that, during the *fitna*, the Umayyads had to fight not only Arab and Berber tribal lords, but also local feudal ones. The paradigmatic example of the latter would be 'Umar ibn Hafsun, the most famous Muwallad rebel, who was active in the area of Málaga and whose ancestry as preserved in Arabic sources links him with Visigothic nobility. For other historians, there is no sound evidence connecting the Muwallad rebels with former Visigothic feudal lords, not even in the case of Ibn Hafsun, whose genealogy can be interpreted as a forgery. On the contrary, what the Muwallad leaders appear to be doing, in the eyes of these historians, is imitating the political behavior of the Arab and Berber rebels of the time.

In the administration, as well as in the army of the Umayyad emirs, the possibility of gaining positions of responsibility and recompense depended on one's status as an Arab or a client, more particularly a client of the Umayyad family. The emir tended to trust his clients, and hence assign the positions of responsibility (and consequently those positions which were the most lucrative) to them; and they were not inclined to admit "competitors" when the ruler's rewards were handed out, least of all when there were few such rewards to go round, resulting in more intense competition. The *fitna* coincided with the moment when the increased rate of conversion must have diminished the amount of income from the taxes paid by non-Muslims. There were attempts to assimilate the two most important Muwallad rebels, Ibn Hafsun and al-Jilliqi, into the Umayyad army. Both suffered ill-treatment during that period, not being allowed to compete on an equal footing with Arabs and clients for the highest honors and stipends in the army. Therefore, they realized the limitations to which their origins subjected them and above all discovered that what the emir offered them was inferior to what they could achieve by acting on their own, as they had done before. In sum, the Muwallads rebelled for their right to share power and compete for economic and social rewards on equal terms with the Arabs and, in the case of converts, with the "old" Muslims. It is important to note that they were not anti-Muslim (except for the last phase of Ibn Hafsun's revolt, and even this is open to doubt). Where the converts first succeeded in fully assimilating themselves was in the religious offices.

From the reign of the emir Muhammad (r. 852–86) to that of 'Abd Allah (r. 888–912) (the latter being 'Abd al-Rahman III's grandfather), Toledo, Zaragoza, and Badajoz in the frontier regions were most of the time independent from Umayyad control. The Umayyads were often reduced to giving support to competing forces against the rebels in power. For example, in the Upper March, the emir Muhammad installed the Arab Tujibi family in order to counteract the influence of the Banu Qasi, a family of local converts whom we have encountered already: they had ties with the Christian kings of the area, and managed to rule independently for almost a century. But the Umayyads saw their rule threatened also in areas near to their capital, Cordoba.

Ibn Hafsun's activities started around the year 878 in the area of Ronda, the mountainous region of Málaga, where he eventually built his stronghold of Bobastro which successfully resisted the attacks and sieges of the Umayyad armies. In 891 Ibn Hafsun threatened Cordoba itself and sought to give political legitimacy to his rebellion by offering his allegiance to the 'Abbasids. He was, however, defeated by the emir 'Abd Allah and although he soon recovered, he never managed to expand further the area under his control. In 899 he is said to have announced his conversion to Christianity, a decision which lost him some of his Muslim supporters and gave the Umayyads the opportunity to present their fight against him as holy war (*jihad*). In 909, Ibn Hafsun is said to have acknowledged the Fatimid caliphate, although when he died in 918, he had returned to Umayyad obedience.

At the beginning of the emirate of 'Abd Allah, civil strife also erupted in Seville, and by 891 the Arabs had seized control of the town, with one local family, the Banu Hajjaj (descendants of Sarah the Goth), emerging as leaders. Ibrahim ibn al-Hajjaj was acknowledged by the Umayyad emir as the king of Seville, where he established his own court.

UMAYYADS AGAINST UMAYYADS: THE REIGN OF THE EMIR 'ABD ALLAH (r. 888–912)

As the disintegration of Umayyad rule accelerated under the reign of the emir 'Abd Allah, the same reign also saw the eruption of violent internal tensions within the Umayyad family. The two processes were obviously related.

'Abd Allah is said to have been behind the death of his brother, al-Mundhir, who had succeeded the emir Muhammad. During his short emirate, al-Mundhir had tried to diminish the influence of some of the most prominent Umayyad client families. Al-Mundhir had also attempted to break the Maliki religious and legal monopoly by supporting other trends, such as those of the Traditionists (*ahl al-hadith*) and the Shafi'is, who insisted that law had to be based on the Qur'an and the Tradition of the Prophet, whereas Andalusi Malikis followed an ongoing juristic tradition, according to their opponents paying too little attention to the sources of revelation. In this context, al-Mundhir was close to Baqi ibn Makhlad (d. 889), a scholar who did not adhere to Malikism and who had brought from his travels to the east new doctrines and legal methodologies. Because of that, Baqi ibn Makhlad suffered persecution by some fanatic Malikis. Al-Mundhir's death put an end to this short-lived attempt at social and religious renewal. 'Abd Allah, who was also accused of having killed his brothers Hisham and al-Qasim, may well have provoked al-Mundhir's death, whose policies he did not follow.

In the year 891, Muhammad, son of the emir 'Abd Allah, gave his father a grandson whose name was 'Abd al-Rahman and who was destined to become the first caliph of al-Andalus. But 'Abd al-Rahman never knew his father. Mutarrif, a son of the emir 'Abd Allah by another wife, killed his half-brother Muhammad twenty days after 'Abd al-Rahman was born.

The reasons for this killing are obscure. Some historians hold 'Abd Allah responsible for the fratricide. The emir suspected that his son Muhammad (whom he may have chosen as his heir) was conspiring against him, perhaps in connection with Ibn Hafsun's presence at the time near Cordoba. Imprisoned, Muhammad was later assassinated by Mutarrif, who beat him to death. For some years, the killer went unpunished. In the year 895, however, the emir 'Abd Allah ordered the execution of his son Mutarrif, again on the grounds that he was conspiring against him. Ibn al-Qutiyya presents Mutarrif as a *zindiq*, a term used for apostates and heretics, meaning that he was executed in accordance with Islamic law. But there is no other evidence that Mutarrif was guilty of either apostasy or heresy, except for his alleged intention to kill some prominent scholars. Ibn al-Qutiyya wrote under 'Abd al-Rahman III as a court historian for whom politics and religion were not and could not be separated: a pretender to the throne was not only a political enemy and a traitor, but also a religious dissident.

'Abd Allah's fear for his life caused him to take unprecedented steps. He had a covered passage built, linking his palace to the near-by Great Mosque of Cordoba. The chronicler 'Arib explains this decision as motivated by the emir's desire to attend the Friday prayer and the rest of prayers, adding that from the passage he could observe the people, meaning those belonging to the Cordoban elites, and keep himself informed of their affairs and their opinions. It is obvious that the passage allowed the emir to move unnoticed from his palace to the mosque, thus diminishing the possibility of assassination. In 910, the emir ordered that a number of members of the Umayyad family should be imprisoned after they had been spotted by the bridge that he had to cross to go hunting. Suspicions that his own family might be acting against him were not unfounded.

In the years 900–1, an Umayyad known as Ibn al-Qitt, a distant relative of the emir, established contact, first, with the Berber tribes settled in the area north of the capital, and next with the Berbers of the area corresponding to modern Extremadura. Ibn al-Qitt preached, made predictions, and performed miracles, while at the same time criticizing the emir 'Abd Allah for his ineptitude and the lack of *jihad* against the Christians, who were expanding the territory under their control in the north of the Iberian peninsula (around this time, the kingdom of Asturias changed its name to León, thus reflecting its territorial expansion). Having gathered many followers, Ibn al-Qitt attacked the town of Zamora, which had been rebuilt and repopulated by Alfonso III in 893. But the Umayyad was eventually defeated by the Christians and his army dispersed.

Ibn al-Qitt was a peculiar rebel and Umayyad pretender. He is said to have been moved to action by a man called Abu 'Ali al-Sarraj, described as an ascetic dressed in white and riding a donkey, who preached *jihad* in the frontier regions of al-Andalus and who had tried to establish an alliance between Ibn Hafsun and the Banu Qasi in the year 898. Nothing more is known about him. The possibility exists that he might have been an Isma'ili, one of those Shi'i agents who were preaching the Isma'ili cause all over the Islamic world at the time and whose presence is attested in al-Andalus during the ninth century. Isma'ili agents were especially active in North Africa. There, an Isma'ili missionary, Abu 'Abd Allah, settled among the Kutama Berbers between 893 and 909 and transformed them into an army that defeated the Aghlabid rulers and led to the establishment of the Fatimid dynasty in Tunis. The first Fatimid caliph adopted the title al-Mahdi in 909. In 901 Ibn al-Qitt had also claimed to be a Mahdi, a messianic figure due to appear at the end of time bringing justice to this world. Abu 'Ali al-Sarraj, like Abu 'Abd Allah, was an ascetic missionary gathering an army among Berber tribesmen in the name of a messianic figure.

But would an Isma'ili agent have elected an Umayyad to be proclaimed Mahdi, a figure who should be a Fatimi, that is a descendant of the Prophet Muhammad though his daughter Fatima? It seems improbable, unless Ibn al-Qitt was a mere pawn in a wider and more complex game, being used in order to aggravate the crisis of the Umayyad emirate and to help with its fall. He would in that case have been discarded afterwards when the true identity of the Mahdi was unveiled, that is, when the Fatimid caliph was proclaimed.

Whatever the agenda behind Abu 'Ali al-Sarraj's activities, the rebellion of Ibn al-Qitt in 901 and the proclamation of the Fatimid caliphate in 909 were severe blows to 'Abd Allah's legitimacy and authority. These blows did not affect him alone. Umayyad rule was under general threat. In order to preserve it, the Umayyad family needed an able and strong leader to unite them, to restore their hold on al-Andalus and to resist the appearance of a dangerous rival, the Fatimid Caliph.

A NEW BEGINNING: 'ABD AL-RAHMAN III BECOMES EMIR (912)

When the emir 'Abd Allah died on 16 October 912, there was no succession crisis. The new emir was his grandson 'Abd al-Rahman, who took seat in the place of honor (*mihrab*) of the hall called al-Kamil (the Perfect) in the royal palace of Cordoba on the very same day. In the presence of his client Badr ibn Ahmad and the prefect of the town Musa ibn Muhammad ibn Sa'id ibn Musa ibn Hudayr, he received the oath of allegiance from his paternal uncles, other Umayyad relatives, the Arabs

who belonged to Quraysh (the Prophet's tribe) and the
Umayyad clients. The jurists and members of the most notable
families of Cordoba followed. Afterwards, 'Abd al-Rahman
made the funeral prayer for his grandfather, who was buried in
the royal cemetery of Cordoba. The oath of allegiance of the
common people was made in the Great Mosque and taken in
the emir's name by the prefect of the town, the judge, and other
high officials. Ibn 'Abd Rabbihi, the court poet, compared the
new emir to the prophet Joseph for his physical beauty, and to
David for his justice and wisdom. His royal seal, like that of his
predecessors 'Abd al-Rahman I and 'Abd al-Rahman II, stated
that " 'Abd al-Rahman is satisfied with God's decision."

Abu l-Mutarrif 'Abd al-Rahman was born in 891, the son of
Muhammad and Muzna, a slave concubine described as
rumiyya, which means that she was a Christian, perhaps from
the north of the peninsula. A maternal uncle, Muzna's brother
Sa'id ibn Abi l-Qasim, held official positions. According to
some sources, 'Abd al-Rahman's grandmother on his father's
side was Oneca or Iñiga, the daughter of Fortún Garcés, who
had become one of the wives of the emir 'Abd Allah. Toda, the
queen of Navarra, claimed on these grounds a family relationship with the Umayyad caliph.

We know almost nothing of 'Abd al-Rahman's childhood
and youth. There is nothing unusual about that, since the
sources do not usually say much, or anything, about the lives of
the rulers before their appearance on the throne. What they
invariably do give us is a description of their looks. Of 'Abd
al-Rahman we are told that he had white skin, dark blue eyes,
and an attractive face. He was also sturdy and a bit chubby. His
legs were short and therefore the stirrups of his saddle were
also quite short. Mounted, the Umayyad appeared tall, but
when he was standing his small stature revealed itself. He used
to dye his beard black.

'Abd al-Rahman's *kunya* was Abu l-Mutarrif (father of Mutarrif), although he is not known to have had any child called Mutarrif. Some modern historians have been surprised by the fact that 'Abd al-Rahman should have used the name of the uncle who killed his father. But among the Andalusi Umayyads the name 'Abd al-Rahman was always accompanied by the *kunya* Abu l-Mutarrif; and it was important for 'Abd al-Rahman III to be associated with his predecessors of the same name, especially the founder of the dynasty, as he was thought to be the new 'Abd al-Rahman who would restore Umayyad power.

'Abd al-Rahman, who was twenty-one years old when his grandfather died, was proclaimed without any opposition on the part of his older relatives, something that was highlighted by the chroniclers as worthy of notice. 'Abd al-Rahman's father Muhammad seems to have been the first-born son of the emir 'Abd Allah and the presumed heir to the throne. But primo-geniture was not what determined succession within the Umayyad family, although there may have been a trend towards it. In any case, 'Abd Allah seems to have preferred his grandson 'Abd al-Rahman to his own surviving children and brothers, even though two of his sons, al-'Asi and Aban, had shown them-selves to be active and capable military leaders. They attended the ceremony in which 'Abd al-Rahman was proclaimed emir and paid him the oath of allegiance, with no reservations recorded. A brother of the dead emir is even described as thanking God on that occasion for having chosen 'Abd al-Rahman as the new emir.

The emir 'Abd Allah had shown his preference by having his grandson live with him in the royal palace, which his sons did not. On some festivals, 'Abd Allah had made 'Abd al-Rahman sit on the royal seat, where he received the salutations of the army. It was said that on his deathbed, 'Abd Allah had given his ring to his grandson, thereby implying that he was naming him his successor. Obviously, 'Abd Allah was deeply suspicious of his own sons, whereas a grandson, given his youth, was easier to keep under control. The high officials of the state (*ahl al-dawla*) may have felt the same. 'Abd al-Rahman III may also have revealed early signs of a personality capable of ensuring the dynasty's survival.

Later on, when 'Abd al-Rahman III proclaimed himself caliph, he mentioned predictions that were circulating about himself. These predictions have not been preserved, but they probably played on the fact that his name coincided with that of the founder of the dynasty and also with that of 'Abd al-Rahman II (the emir who had brought the Umayyads up to date through the assimilation of 'Abbasid ruling practices and the support given to an emergent scholarly class). Also, was 'Abd al-Rahman III not the grandson of an Umayyad ruler, as 'Abd al-Rahman I had been the grandson of the Umayyad caliph Hisham, their respective fathers having died prematurely?

'Abd al-Rahman III was also the eighth Umayyad emir. His rival, the Fatimid caliph, belonged to the Isma'ili Shi'is, those who believed that the Imams follow one another in cycles of seven, like the days of the week. Could the Umayyads have been influenced by this belief? Had not the Umayyad caliphs of Damascus numbered fourteen before their fall? The emir 'Abd Allah could easily have been seen as representing the end of a cycle of seven Umayyad emirs in al-Andalus. The time was then ripe for a new 'Abd al-Rahman to appear who would open a new cycle of power and prosperity for the dynasty. The fact that 'Abd al-Rahman III's close collaborator in the early part of his reign was called Badr goes in the same direction, as 'Abd al-Rahman I's success in al-Andalus owed much to the energy and devotion of his own manumitted slave Badr. That predictions of a new 'Abd al-Rahman circulated in al-Andalus at the time is also shown by the fact that 'Umar ibn Hafsun's biography was constructed along the lines of that of 'Abd al-Rahman I. The latter had been in his twenties when he became the first Umayyad emir of al-Andalus, so that a new 'Abd al-Rahman ought not be much older.

If his family and the Cordoban elites presented a united front at the proclamation ceremony, this does not mean that there was no room for trouble both then and later. The new emir ordered that Musa ibn Ziyad be imprisoned. This man belonged to a family of Arab notables, had been vizier under 'Abd Allah and had always shown enmity towards 'Abd al-Rahman. Musa ibn Ziyad stayed in prison from 912 until 919, when he was executed together with other notables accused of disloyal behavior towards the emir.

SECURING THE CENTRAL LANDS AND THE DEFEAT OF THE HAFSUNIDS (912–28)

The case of Musa ibn Ziyad apart, 'Abd al-Rahman III seems to have had the support of the families who had served the Umayyads during the previous century and who had a vested interest in the survival of the dynasty. For a while, he kept most of the high officials in the positions to which they had been appointed by his grandfather. He thus confirmed his clients Musa ibn Muhammad ibn Sa'id ibn Musa ibn Hudayr as prefect of the town, 'Abd Allah ibn Muhammad al-Zajjali as secretary, and Ahmad ibn Muhammad ibn Abi 'Abda as military commander. The latter, who had led many campaigns against 'Umar ibn Hafsun during the reign of 'Abd Allah, was dismissed on December of the same year, to be reappointed shortly afterwards. He died in 917 fighting against the northern Christians. As for Ibn Hudayr, he was dismissed in 915, but served 'Abd al-Rahman III in different capacities during the following years, until in 921 he was appointed chamberlain (*hajib*). Al-Zajjali was dismissed before his death in 914, although his relatives continued to serve the emir.

As soon as he was proclaimed emir, letters were sent to the governors of the districts asking for their oaths of allegiance. The first answer, a chronicle claims, came from the governor of Martos (in the district of Jaén), whose Arab name, Sa'id ibn al-Salim, evoked the ideas of happiness, health, and peace. This was understood as a good omen for the new emir.

'Abd al-Rahman III's priority was to restore Umayyad control over the territories near his capital, and thus until the year 920 he did not lead personally any military campaign in the frontier regions. The new emir needed to achieve military success in order to strengthen his legitimacy and justify the choice made by his grandfather. It was some time before he dared to lead a military expedition in person.

During the year 912, he sent some military commanders against the rebel Berbers north of Cordoba. One of the Berber leaders was killed and his head sent to Cordoba. On 24 November 912, the rebel's head was hung on the Bab al-Sudda gate of the royal palace, the first of many to follow.

Another expedition was sent against the rebels in the district of Cabra, a town not far from Cordoba. Nearby Ecija was conquered by the chamberlain Badr on 1st January 913 without any bloodshed. The walls were destroyed, but the castle was kept and a governor belonging to the Banu Basil family, clients of the Umayyads, was appointed by the emir. On 13 January, it is recorded that the emir had a hunting day at one of his villas and returned to Cordoba in the evening, with a lavish parade that was intended for public consumption.

Shortly after, the emir was ready to lead an expedition himself in the provinces of Jaén and Granada, situated to the southeast of Cordoba. But the emir first took some preparatory

steps. In January 913 a rebel from Jaén, who had been imprisoned during the reign of 'Abd Allah, was freed under the
promise that he would not rebel again. Presumably, he was
allowed to return to his area of influence in order to support
the emir's expedition. But he did rebel again, was made prisoner, and crucified.

In February, letters instructed the governors to recruit soldiers and gather equipment and provisions. The first to answer
was the army of Damascus, settled in the region of Granada.
Their judge, the Arab 'Abd Allah ibn Muhammad ibn 'Abd
al-Khaliq al-Ghassani, who seems to have been a scholar rather
than a soldier, obtained the obedience of his fellow soldiers,
and thanks to them the emir had troops to start his first campaign. It is not clear whether the emir had named him judge of
Granada before or after the pledge of obedience by the army of
Damascus.

On 17 April 913, corresponding to the sacred month of
Ramadan, when Muslims have to perform the obligatory fast,
the emir left Cordoba, and many fortresses in the district of
Jaén and Granada were conquered and loyal governors
appointed. Their rebel lords swore obedience to the emir,
received immunity from punishment (aman) and were sent
with their families to Cordoba. Part of the area where this
campaign took place had until then been under the control of
Ibn Hafsun and his allies. Ibn Hafsun counter-attacked, threat-
ening the capital of the district of Granada, but the population
of the town, aware that part of the emir's army was on its way,
fought him, killing many of his men.

On 25 May 913, the emir attacked Juviles, one of the most
impregnable fortresses of Ibn Hafsun, where Christians who
had managed to escape from the other conquered fortresses
had taken refuge. Juviles eventually surrendered and the
Christian refugees were handed to the emir, who had all of

them beheaded. After conquering other fortresses, 'Abd al-Rahman III returned to Cordoba, where he entered on 18 July 913, a symbolic day, as it coincided with the Festival of the Sacrifice that signals the end of the pilgrimage to Mecca. His first campaign had thus started with a sacred month, that of fast, and ended with another, that of pilgrimage.

The historian Ibn Hayyan states that no king had ever been known to conquer so many fortresses (the symbolic number seventy is given by the sources) in just one campaign. The court poet Ibn 'Abd Rabbihi praised 'Abd al-Rahman III to the skies, comparing him to Solomon and Alexander. It was undoubtedly a promising start, but the emir was still unable at the time to exercise complete control of the conquered area with his own men. In fact, some of the rebel lords who accompanied him back to Cordoba were allowed to return to their old fortresses, indicating that control of the territory could only be ensured by them, and this only as long as they remained obedient to the emir. Nor were those who stayed in Cordoba always to be trusted. One Habil ibn Habil, for example, escaped in 914 and returned to his fortress of Esteban. The emir had to send his commander Ibn Abi 'Abda against him.

On 7 August 913, the de facto independent ruler of Seville, 'Abd al-Rahman ibn Ibrahim ibn Hajjaj, died and the succession led to division among his relatives. His brother Muhammad, who had ruled the town of Carmona, offered 'Abd al-Rahman III his help to fight Ahmad ibn Maslama, whom the people of Seville had elected as their ruler. Seville was besieged for several months and in December 913, it was conquered by the chamberlain Badr. The walls, which had been built by 'Abd al-Rahman II after the Viking attack, were destroyed and a loyal governor was appointed.

In the spring of 914, the emir led his second campaign, this time against Ibn Hafsun's fortresses in the area of Málaga. The chronicles describe the ruler's army as behaving with great cruelty during the campaign of the year 914, especially during the attack against the fortress of Turrush, where the destruction of the land and the killing of men were ferocious. There, some of Ibn Hafsun's followers were Christians and the heads of those killed were sent to Cordoba as trophies. In Algeciras, the ships belonging to Ibn Hafsun that brought provisions from North Africa (probably from the Fatimids, with whom Ibn Hafsun had established contact) were all destroyed. During the same campaign, the emir traversed the districts of Sidonia, Morón, and Carmona. This town was besieged. Its rebel lord, Habib ibn Sawada, surrendered and was granted safeguard, leaving for Cordoba with his family. He would rebel again in 917. Defeated, Habib and two of his sons were imprisoned in Cordoba in the famous underground prison of the royal palace. They were executed in 919 together with Musa ibn Ziyad.

A new campaign in the district of Málaga took place in 915, led by Aban, a paternal uncle of the emir, who died shortly afterwards at the age of fifty-five. But the main event of that year and the next was a famine provoked by a severe drought. Prayers asking for rain led by the director of the Friday prayer, the famous jurist Muhammad ibn 'Umar ibn Lubaba, were unsuccessful. His rival and enemy Ahmad ibn Muhammad ibn Ziyad led the prayer for rain on 1st May and it brought some rain that saved part of the harvest. Prices, however, increased all over al-Andalus, affecting both the emir's territories and those of the rebels. The death toll was terrible in all social strata. The poor died in such numbers that many corpses were lying unburied. Many notables also died in Cordoba and in other towns. The emir and some of his men, such as his chamberlain Badr, increased their almsgiving, and the chronicles recorded this as proof of their piety. It was then that Ibn Hafsun asked for peace and was given safeguard; he maintained obedience to the emir until his death in 918.

By 917, the armies of the emir were venturing farther from Cordoba, with campaigns in the eastern Mediterranean districts (Tudmir and Valencia) and in the Gharb (western Andalucía, near Portugal), where Niebla was conquered.

Ibn Hafsun died in the year 918. Although he had kept his obedience to the Umayyad emir, official chronicles refer to him in extremely derogatory terms (apostate, leader of the infidels, head of the hypocrites, refuge of dissidents and heretics), and single him out among the other rebels, indicating how dangerous he was considered to be. His death was therefore seen as a divine sign announcing the end of his abominable rebellion. It did indeed bring discord among his sons. One of them, Sulayman, was defeated in the district of Granada and brought to Cordoba, where he lived for some time before rebelling again.

In May 919, the emir led what was known as the campaign of Belda in the district of Málaga. The Muslims of the fortress asked for safe-conduct and having obtained it, they abandoned Belda and went to the emir's camp. But the Christians refused to surrender. Defeated, they were almost all killed. Some of their notables were made prisoners and brought to the emir, who ordered them to be beheaded. More than a hundred and seventy heads were gathered. A military display was then made in front of the walls of Bobastro, the most emblematic fortress of the Hafsunids, and its lord, Ja'far ibn 'Umar ibn Hafsun (who claimed to have converted to Christianity, although he was later accused of being a crypto-Muslim), agreed to pay tribute. The emir returned to Cordoba in June 919.

In October 920, Ja'far ibn 'Umar ibn Hafsun was killed in Bobastro by some Christians, and his brother Sulayman became its new lord. Another brother, 'Abd al-Rahman ibn 'Umar ibn

Hafsun, who had fallen out with Ja'far, lord of Bobastro, ruled Turrush. In 921, this fortress was also conquered by the emir and after his defeat, this 'Abd al-Rahman settled in Cordoba where he earned his living working as a copyist. A mosque was built in the site of the church of Turrush.

Fighting against the remaining rebels continued in the following years in the areas of Priego, Granada, and Málaga, while at the same time the emir inspected those areas, such as Seville and Carmona, that were already under his control. The maritime town of Pechina (Almería) became integrated into the Umayyad state.

In 923, Bobastro was attacked. Some of its inhabitants, including the bishop Ibn Maqsim, were in favor of coming to terms with the emir. But having discovered their plans, Sulayman ibn 'Umar ibn Hafsun tortured and killed the suspects. During this campaign, the Umayyad army is described as crossing mountainous land that had never before been traversed. Many Hafsunid fortresses were partially destroyed. The next campaign took place in 925 and it marked the end of the rebellion in the districts of Jaén and Granada, where some of those who had pledged obedience had rebelled again. Military victory was followed by a policy of destruction of rebel strongholds and redistribution of the population in the plains.

In 926 Sulayman ibn 'Umar ibn Hafsun was killed and was succeeded by his brother Hafs. The emir led the last campaign against Bobastro in May 927. After besieging the Hafsunid fortress, the emir moved to the east, conquering the neighboring castles of Olías, Santopitar, Comares and Jotrón, inhabited exclusively by Christians who received help from the coast, possibly a reference to Fatimid support. Having eliminated any possibility of military aid or refuge, the emir returned to Bobastro where he strengthened the siege by building a rival fortress. After his return to Cordoba in August 927, he was

informed of the fall of Bobastro on 17 January 928 with the surrender of Hafs. The son of 'Umar ibn Hafsun moved with his
family to Cordoba, where he entered the army as mercenary.

THE FRONTIER REGIONS

When 'Abd al-Rahman became emir, he sent trusted men to
the governors of the frontier regions with letters in which they
were asked to return an official document recording their oath
of allegiance. The first to answer was the lord of Zaragoza,
Muhammad ibn 'Abd al-Rahman al-Tujibi. A chronicle suggests
that every region responded, thus implying that 'Abd
al-Rahman's rule all over those lands was acknowledged.

The situation in the frontier area was far from being one of
obedience. Most of the lords were acting independently from
Cordoba, engaging in fights against each other and against the
Christians, with shifting allegiances across the borders of religious affiliations.

In the upper frontier, the most important lineages were
those of the Muwallad Banu Qasi and the Arab Tujibids. The latter had settled in the area by the middle of the ninth century
with Umayyad support in order to check the power of the Banu
Qasi, whose political and military power can be traced back to
the eighth century. During the early years of 'Abd al-Rahman
III's reign, the confrontation between the Banu Qasi and the
Tujibids was accompanied by violent conflicts within those lineages. At the same time, they were also involved in the fight
against the Christians, especially the new kings of Navarra.

The area of Santaver was under the control of the Berber
Banu Dhi l-Nun, who had extended their dominion to the eastern Mediterranean coast. Like the Tujibis, this and other Berber
lineages were to become independent ruling lineages in their

respective domains when the Umayyad caliphate collapsed at the beginning of the eleventh century.

Toledo may have been occupied briefly by the Asturian-Leonese king Alfonso III before his death in 910. Later on, the town, famous for its resistance to Umayyad control, was ruled by a man called Lubb ibn Tarbisha. To the west of Toledo, there were Berber settlements beyond the reach of Cordoban rule, as the episode of Ibn al-Qitt's messianic movement reveals. The initial aim of that movement had been to reconquer Zamora from Christian hands, as the kings of León managed to expand their control in the Duero valley in the ninth to the tenth centuries, and to advance toward the Tajo river.

In the Lower March, in what is now known as Extremadura, the area of Badajoz was in the hands of al-Jilliqi and his descendants, whereas in Mérida the Berber Banu Tajit acted as independent lords. In 913, Ordoño II (the future king of León, r. 914–24), acting as king of Galicia, had launched a campaign in Extremadura, attacking Evora. The walls of this town were in such disrepair that the Christians were able to sack the town, killing its men and taking prisoner the women and children. The Muslims are said to have reacted by strengthening their fortresses, but two years later Ordoño II made another incursion in the area without meeting much resistance. The Tajo frontier thus seems to have lacked a proper defensive system, allowing the Christians to penetrate the area with relative ease.

The first campaign in the frontier regions ordered by the emir took place in 916. In July, the commander Ibn Abi 'Abda attacked unspecified Christian territory and took prisoners and booty. In 917, joined by people of the frontier, he besieged the fortress of San Esteban de Gormaz, but the Christians came in its defence and Ibn Abi 'Abda and other Muslims died as martyrs. Interestingly, the tenth-century Cordoban historian

'Arib notes that some of the people of the frontier behaved as
religious hypocrites, presumably meaning that they sided with
the invaders and that their conduct helped the Christians defeat
the Muslims (some years later, in 939, we shall see that the
caliph 'Abd al-Rahman III was the victim of similar behavior on
the part of the people of the frontier). In June 918, Ordoño II
and Sancho, king of Pamplona, acted together against the
Muslims in the area of Nájera and Tudela, with Sancho's troops
attacking the fortress of Valtierra and burning its mosque.

Christian offensive moves were clearly related to the
Umayyad weakness, but the death of Ibn Hafsun and the conflict between his sons seems to have helped, for in 918 and 919,
there were successful summer campaigns organized from
Cordoba against the Christians, led by Umayyad commanders.
Soon the emir decided to take things into his own hands, and in
920 he led the campaign of Muez in person. He crossed the
central frontier and the lord of Toledo joined him, to be
rewarded by having his lordship acknowledged by the emir. But
the lords of the region of Guadalajara, the Berber Banu Salim,
were removed, and the emir appointed a governor and a judge.
'Abd al-Rahman III then went to the fortress of Medinaceli,
destined to play a crucial role in Umayyad frontier policies. He
pretended that he was going in the direction of the Upper
March, but moved instead to the area of al-Qila' (the Castles),
Alava, and Navarra. His commander, the Qurashi Sa'id ibn
al-Mundhir, was sent to Osma, which he attacked by surprise
and demolished, moving afterwards against San Esteban de
Gormaz and Clunia. This area was part of the expanding region
of Castille, whose count around 930 was Fernán González. The
county of Castille acquired during the tenth century an increasing importance as a militarized society organized for war
against the Muslims. At the time of the 920 campaign, signs of
an ebullient society were already evident. For his part, the emir

moved to Muslim Tudela in order to protect it against King Sancho, and then to Calahorra, a Muslim fortress that had been captured by the Christians and then abandoned. The Muslim army crossed the Ebro river and fought against the Christian soldiers of Kings Ordoño and Sancho, who were acting together. The latter were defeated on 25 July 920. On 29 July, the castle of Muez, where some had taken refuge, was conquered. Muslim sources state that five hundred Christians were killed and their heads brought to Cordoba. In Atienza, the emir distributed precious clothing and riding animals to the people of the frontier who had fought with him.

But events taking place in 923 obliged the emir to intervene on the frontier again. After his victorious battle of Viguera, the king of Navarra, Sancho Garcés, captured members of the Banu Qasi and of the Berber Banu Dhi l-Nun families and killed them. As they had all of them remained obedient to the Umayyad emir in the fortresses where they ruled, 'Abd al-Rahman III took immediate measures. He sent one of his commanders to the frontier to support the Muslims there. The emir intervened personally in 924 in the Pamplona campaign, when the capital of the kingdom of Navarra was attacked and sacked. Traversing the eastern regions of Tudmir and Valencia, he obtained the submission of rebel lords. Then he reached the Upper Frontier, where he was joined by the Tujibis, whose rule he had formally acknowledged. The Umayyad emir's reactions seem to indicate that he felt obliged to help those lords of the frontier who had sworn allegiance to him in exchange for acknowledging their rule.

From 924 until 928, the emir concentrated mainly on the battle against the Hafsunids, but he did send 'Abd al-Hamid ibn Basil on a campaign in the Middle Frontier in 926, with the result that taxes were collected in the area of Santaver, where the Banu Dhi l-Nun had been ruling independently. After the fall of Bobastro, the Berber territories along the Guadiana and Mérida were conquered.

As the poet Ibn 'Abd Rabbihi said, the emir had succeeded in uniting "the divided community," lifting "the obscure coverings of darkness from it." The moment had arrived to illuminate that community with the light of the caliphate.

4

CALIPHATE AND
CONSOLIDATION (929–61)

The South winds are only remotely related to his beneficence,
    while the clouds are shamed by his generosity;
In his face there is evidence of [God's] light, whereas the kissing
    of his hand is a religious sacrifice to God.

            Ibn 'Abd Rabbihi (transl. J.T. Monroe)

THE ADOPTION OF THE CALIPHAL TITLE AND THE MINTING OF GOLD

On Friday 16 January 929, the first day of Dhu l-Hijja, the month when the pilgrimage to Mecca takes place, 'Abd al-Rahman III proclaimed himself Commander of the Faithful (*amir al-mu'minin*), thereby identifying himself as the caliph (*khalifa*), God's representative on earth through the inheritance of the Prophet Muhammad who had acted both as the religious and political leader (imam) of the community of believers established by him in Medina.

The official preachers referred to 'Abd al-Rahman III as Commander of the Faithful in the sermon at the Friday prayer, and the emir was addressed by this title from then onwards. He also adopted two regnal titles. The most widely reported in the sources is *al-Nasir li-din Allah* (he who brings victory to God's religion), also found in inscriptions and on coins. The other title will be dealt with below.

The Umayyad emirs of al-Andalus had not dared until then to proclaim themselves caliphs, and consequently they did not mint gold, although they claimed the inheritance of their ancestors, the Umayyads of Damascus, which entitled them to rule. At the same time, the Andalusi Umayyads did not acknowledge the 'Abbasid caliphs, who had put an end to the Umayyad caliphate and massacred most members of their family.

For more than a century al-Andalus had thus been a sort of "no man's land" over the issue of the imam or legitimate political and religious leader of the Muslim community, as it would be again under the Party kings, when an unidentified and ambiguous " *'abd Allah amir al-mu'minin*" (the Servant of God, the Commander of the Faithful) was acknowledged as imam. If this looked problematic from a theoretical point of view, as the imam of the Muslim community was supposed to be a real person, in practice it does not seem to have been so, and no Andalusi scholar is recorded as having felt the need to write about it. In reality, it was the best solution to a political and religious problem. As for the Andalusi Umayyads, the 'Abbasids were usurpers of the legitimate Umayyad caliphate. The latter would be restored one day, but as long as the descendants of the legitimate caliphs were not strong enough to reclaim their inherit-ance in the central Islamic lands, especially by ruling the holy places of Mecca and Medina, the adoption of the caliphal title had to be postponed.

Why then did 'Abd al-Rahman III feel that the moment had come to claim this caliphal inheritance? There were several reasons, related both to external and internal circumstances. On the one hand, there was the devaluation of the title by the weakening power of the 'Abbasids themselves and the appearance of a second caliphate in North Africa, that of the Fatimids. On the other hand, the defeat of the Hafsunids and the regaining of Umayyad control over most of Andalusi territory was a triumph similar to that achieved by 'Abd al-Rahman I when he became emir, but the new 'Abd al-Rahman could now assert his right to the caliphate.

The 'Abbasids still ruled as caliphs in Baghdad, but their power was greatly diminished and territorially reduced. The first part of 'Abd al-Rahman III's reign coincided with that of al-Muqtadir bi-llah (r. 908–32), who had become caliph when he was only thirteen, an age that according to the legal requirements made doubtful his appointment as caliph and that, in any case, opened room for trouble (as it would when 'Abd al-Rahman's III's grandson, Hisham II, became caliph at the age of eleven). Al-Muqtadir was deposed twice during his reign by rival 'Abbasid candidates and showed political and military weakness. The Karmatis, a radical Shi'i group related to the Isma'ilis, were able to plunder Mecca in 928, carrying off the Black Stone. This event caused great scandal and sorrow all over the Islamic world. In al-Andalus a woman was reported not to have laughed from that date until she died in 931. Al-Muqtadir's successors had very short reigns, being puppets in the hands of the Turkish troops. During the reign of the 'Abbasid caliph al-Muqtadir, the rival caliphate of the Fatimids was established in North Africa. The Fatimids claimed to be endowed with charismatic powers and supernatural knowledge owing to their direct descent from the Prophet through 'Ali, his cousin and son-in-law, and his daughter Fatima. In the early period of their rule, they also stressed eschatological expectations. The first caliph (r. 909–34) was known as *al-Mahdi*, the messianic title with a long tradition among the Shi'is, which we have encountered as the title adopted by the Umayyad pretender Ibn al-Qitt. The second Fatimid caliph

(r. 934–46) adopted another messianic title, *al-Qa'im bi-amr Allah* (the one who stands up for God's order). He was already known by that title in 912, when he was named heir to the throne. This was in order to counteract the proclamation of a rival *Mahdi* by the Berber Kutama, who were dissatisfied with the policies of the Fatimid imam who bore that name and whom they had helped become caliph. By 944, the Fatimid dynasty was seriously threatened by the appearance of a Khariji Berber rebel, Abu Yazid, known as the Man of the Donkey, who sought Umayyad support and was eventually defeated by the third Fatimid caliph (r. 946–53), who, as a consequence, adopted the caliphal title *al-Mansur* (the victor). 'Abd al-Rahman III's reign also coincided with that of the fourth Fatimid caliph, al-Mu'izz (r. 953–75), during whose reign eschatological expectations started to be played down.

Ibn Hazm stated that 'Abd al-Rahman III adopted the same caliphal title, *al-Qa'im bi-amr Allah* (with the variant *al-qa'im bi-llah*, he who stands up for God), borne by the second Fatimid caliph, and that he saw that title being used in caliphal letters written from Madinat al-Zahra'. Other sources fail to mention this title, although the formula *al-qa'im bi-l-haqq* (he who stands up for Truth) appears in a letter sent by 'Abd al-Rahman III to his North African allies. The adoption of the title *al-Qa'im* reflects a stage when the Umayyad was clearly trying to rival the Fatimids in their claims to divine proximity and charismatic powers, a stage that is to be connected with the building of Madinat al-Zahra', a town that, as we shall see, embodies an eschatological message. When this message ceased to be functional, the messianic title also lost its relevance and must have become a source of embarrassment, as a too obvious echo of Fatimid claims to legitimacy.

In fact, the obvious link between the appearance of the Fatimid caliphate and the subsequent Umayyad claim to it is never mentioned in the Andalusi sources, whereas they do relate it to the decline of the 'Abbasid caliphate. Rivalry with a heretical caliphate did not add any credit to the Sunni Umayyads. By contrast, 'Abbasid inability to cater for the religious and political needs of the Islamic community was a good reason for the Umayyads to claim the Sunni caliphate.

There were also internal circumstances behind the caliphal proclamation. When it took place in 929, 'Abd al-Rahman III had not yet achieved effective control of all Andalusi territory. In fact, he would spend the following years trying to bring the frontier regions under his rule. What he had achieved was the defeat of the rebels in the central lands of al-Andalus, especially the defeat of the Hafsunids. In the preceding years, predictions announcing the end of Arab-Muslim rule in al-Andalus had been circulating both among Christians and Muslims, and Ibn Hafsun and his sons surely made political use of them. Some months before his proclamation as caliph, in March 928, 'Abd al-Rahman III visited Bobastro and fasted during the time he spent there. The chroniclers describe the impregnable location of the fortress in order to emphasize the merits of its conquest. Churches were demolished. The emir exhumed the graves of Ibn Hafsun and his son, allegedly revealing that they had been buried as Christians, although there are reasonable doubts about whether Ibn Hafsun and his son had really died as non-Muslims. Their corpses were hung in Cordoba together with the corpse of another son of Ibn Hafsun. They stayed there for a long time, until the river Guadalquivir flooded in 942 and swept them away. Their punishment after death had been predicted some years before by a well known poet.

Part of Ibn Hafsun's biography can be interpreted as a "re-creation" of the biography of 'Abd al-Rahman I, depicting the Muwallad rebel as the new conqueror of al-Andalus and the founder of a new dynasty, in what appears as a sort of messianic characterization. From the point of view of his opponents, Ibn Hafsun was a new pharaoh, the embodiment of the proud, insolent tyrant who claims divinity and who damns himself through his vanity and pride. His defeat was, therefore, a momentous victory, one that revealed the exceptional nature of the emir who had made it possible, an emir who was therefore entitled to be a caliph. As the poet Ibn 'Abd Rabbihi put it, rebellion and apostasy predominated in al-Andalus "until we were given in rescue, like a light putting heaven and earth next to each other, the Caliph of God, whom He elected and chose over all creation."

The sources are silent regarding how the decision of restoring the Umayyad caliphate was taken, who was behind it, and what the reaction of both the elites (especially the jurists) and the common people was. According to the eleventh-century Cordoban author Ibn Hazm, caliphs could be named in three different ways: by nomination by a previous caliph, use of force, and nomination by an assembly (shura). The last was the method followed in 'Abd al-Rahman III's case. The shura method had been first used by the second caliph, 'Umar ibn al-Khattab, to choose his successor in Medina. 'Uthman ibn 'Affan, the Umayyads' ancestor, was the candidate elected, although he, like his predecessors, was rejected by the Shi'is. Shi'is, in fact, deny the possibility that God could have left to the Muslim community the choice of their imam. According to the Shi'is, the Prophet had named his cousin and son-in-law 'Ali ibn Abi Talib as his successor, and therefore Abu Bakr, 'Umar, and 'Uthman, the first caliphs, were not legitimate rulers. Direct nomination by the Prophet and, subsequently, nomination by the previous imam within the Prophet's family in an uninterrupted way, ensured that the leader was legitimate.

One of the prerogatives of the caliphs was the minting of gold. From the 890s and until 928, there had been symptoms of a monetary crisis in al-Andalus, as shown by the near total disappearance of currency. This was a reflection of the political and fiscal crisis of the Umayyad emirate during that period. Shortly before his proclamation as caliph, in November 928, ‘Abd al-Rahman III ordered the creation of a mint in Cordoba, where not only silver currency was coined, as his predecessors had done before him, but also gold. The silver coin (dirham) continued to be the basic mainstay of the monetary system, since gold coins (dinar) were not minted on a yearly basis. A chronicler described this step taken by the emir as "bringing great benefit to the people and fulfilling the prerogatives of his state."

Minting in gold was the clearest proclamation of the new concept of Umayyad power leading to the adoption of the caliphal title. Until then, Aghlabid dinars had circulated in the Iberian peninsula. After the collapse of this North African dynasty which acknowledged the ‘Abbasid caliphate, the Fatimids started minting gold and silver coins that proclaimed their imamate. These dinars and dirhams were not acceptable to the Umayyads, and if they could not stop their circulation, they could counter their slogans with their own. Thus, Umayyad coins proclaimed the rule of "the servant of God ‘Abd al-Rahman, Commander of the Faithful, who brings victory to God's religion."

Caliphal coins evolved in their design through various phases, until a fairly specific model was arrived at. Fraudulent practices were punished. Certain changes are associated with the relocation of the mint in 947 from Cordoba to Madinat al-Zahra’, among them, the appearance of rich vegetal and floral ornamentation. We shall see the causes of this development when dealing with the meaning of Madinat al-Zahra’ and the religious policies of ‘Abd al-Rahman III.

The minting of dinars by both the Fatimids and the Umayyads increased the need for gold. It was especially abundant in West Africa, and Saharan trade, whether in slaves or gold, flourished. At Sijilmasa, a town situated in the fringes of the Sahara, the gold entered the commercial network of North Africa. The tenth-century traveller and geographer Ibn Hawqal, who was also a Fatimid spy, recorded telling anecdotes about the extraordinary size and value of that network and the wealth of the rulers and merchants of Sijilmasa. In 953, the Midrarid ruler of this town even proclaimed himself caliph, the first Berber prince to have gone so far. For his part, a Berber rebel against the Fatimids, Abu Yazid, the "Man of the Donkey," when he conquered Qayrawan in 944, minted gold coins with a Khariji slogan. Gold and caliphate went hand in hand, and the North African trade routes were the key to the former.

EXTENDING UMAYYAD POWER IN THE FRONTIER REGIONS: THE FALL OF TOLEDO AND ZARAGOZA

'Abd al-Rahman III's proclamation as caliph was followed by a severe drought in al-Andalus, not an auspicious beginning, as it caused prices to rise. Prayers for rain were said in the Cordoba mosque and in the open-air oratories, as well as in the other districts, but they were not successful.

The years 928–9 saw the extension of caliphal rule in the western part of al-Andalus and along the Lower March, an area where in the preceding years there had been numerous conflicts among the local lords. One of 'Abd al-Rahman III's commanders conquered Mérida and Santarén. The caliph himself led the campaign against Badajoz in May 929. Beja and Badajoz eventually surrendered (930–1) and, following the usual practice, their lords with their families were sent to Cordoba, where some were enrolled in the army. The lord of Ocsonoba, for his part, was allowed to stay in his town, ruling now in the name of the caliph.

The Middle March was a crucial area for communication between north and south and west and east, and its control was vital for the Umayyads. We have already mentioned that the Cordoban emirs had never been able to consolidate their rule over Toledo, whose population was famous for its tendency to rebel against Cordoba. By 930, however, the area surrounding Toledo had become loyalist territory. There were Umayyad governors in Calatrava, Talamanca, Madrid, and Talavera, and the Berber Banu Dhi l-Nun had also pledged obedience to the caliph. The latter then sent some trusted officials and some jurists to convince the Toledans to acknowledge his rule and to pay taxes. Failing to respond positively, an army was sent against them in May 930. A town, called "the City of victory," was built opposite Toledo in order to carry out a siege that must have been foreseen as long and difficult, and in fact it lasted until 932. The resistance of the Toledans might have lasted longer had they been able to secure Christian help. Famine eventually led them to surrender but even so, they were still able to demand favorable conditions from the victors. The Toledans insisted that they were not to pay taxes other than the legal tenth (*zakat*) and not to host troops in their homes, and that they were to keep their own director of prayer and be ruled by their own leaders. When the caliph accepted these conditions of the Toledans, the gates of the town were opened for him. A citadel was built inside Toledo for the Umayyad representative and his troops, surrounded by high walls that isolated it from the rest of the town. The defeated were thus granted a wide space of autonomy, and the caliph was forced to accommodate himself to local power. In spite of its shortcomings from the point of view of caliphal authority, or perhaps because of them, the end of the Toledan rebellion was celebrated in

Cordoba with a lavish banquet offered by the caliph to all those who had taken part in the conquest, a celebration that coincided with the circumcision of some of his sons.

The next aim of the caliph was the Upper Frontier. Between 924 and 933 there were internecine disputes among the local lineages controlling the area, with the Banu Qasi seriously weakened. By 930 Zaragoza was ruled by Muhammad ibn Hashim al-Tujibi. When he succeeded his father as lord of Zaragoza, the caliph showed his displeasure at this inheritance of offices that ignored his right of appointing his representatives in a territory that was, at least in theory, under his rule.

In 934 'Abd al-Rahman III decided to lead an expedition against the Christians, known as the campaign of Osma, but Muhammad ibn Hashim al-Tujibi and the lords of Huesca and Barbastro refused to join him, whereas the Tujibi rulers of Calatayud and Daroca accepted. 'Abd al-Rahman III then attacked the rebels and Muhammad ibn Hashim al-Tujibi had to submit, joining the expedition and handing over some of his castles to the Umayyad. The Muslim army then attacked Ramiro II, causing great damage in his territory.

As Muhammad ibn Hashim al-Tujibi rebelled again, in 935 the caliph signed a treaty with the king of León in order to ensure that Zaragoza could not count on Christian help. The Tujibi lords of Calatayud and Daroca maintained their loyalty to 'Abd al-Rahman III and some fortresses around Zaragoza were put under Umayyad control. The submission of the capital of the Upper Frontier seemed to be approaching when the caliph returned to Cordoba, leaving his commanders in charge of the siege, probably unaware of the troubles ahead.

Between 935 and 936, Ramiro II broke the treaty with the caliph, the count of Barcelona attacked the Umayyad army along the frontier, the Banu Dhi l-Nun rebelled, and the lords of Calatayud and Daroca joined their relative, the lord of

Zaragoza, against the caliph. This widespread disaffection seems to have been linked with the presence in the area of Ahmad ibn Ishaq al-Qurashi.

This man belonged to a family of descendants of Marwan I (r. 684–5, the fourth Umayyad caliph of Damascus), who had settled in Seville. They thought of themselves as equals of the ruling Umayyad family, whom they had helped in their bid for power. In the second half of the ninth century, some of them had joined in the Sevillan rebellion against the emir 'Abd Allah and moved to Cordoba when the Sevillans surrendered to 'Abd al-Rahman III in 913, entering the service of the caliph as military commanders, governors, and viziers. Ahmad ibn Ishaq took part in the siege of Zaragoza, but the caliph became suspicious of his activities and in 936 he was dismissed and executed. His brother Umayya rebelled in Santarén and sought an alliance with the Christians, being defeated in 939.

The caliph decided to lead himself the punitive campaign against Zaragoza. Part of his troops, under the command of Durri, freedman of the caliph, attacked Talavera and the Berber territory of Nafza, in the Middle March, where rebellion had broken again. The caliph, in the meantime, conquered Calatayud and Daroca, and their Tujibi lords were killed. Mutarrif ibn Mundhir al-Tujibi, lord of Calatayud, had obtained help from the northern Christians. The caliph had written to him condemning this behavior and ordering him to cut his links with the unbelievers, but Mutarrif's answer was: "how would I cut my right hand with my left hand?," meaning that the Christians were his right hand and the caliph his left hand. This answer caused great scandal among Muslims, and the conquest of Calatayud by the caliphal troops was particularly bloody.

The siege of Zaragoza lasted eight months during the years 936–7, when a new drought was devastating the peninsula. On

23 August 937, Zaragoza surrendered, although the negoti-
ations lasted until November. A document was finally produced,
establishing that Muhammad b. Hashim al-Tujibi was to aban-
don the town with his relatives and settle as governor in
another town on the frontier for some time. The new governor
of Zaragoza, appointed by the caliph, had to treat well those
Tujibis who stayed behind in the town and had to settle in an
area far from their residences in order to avoid conflicts. When
the period established by the caliph ended, Muhammad ibn
Hashim al-Tujibi had to go to Cordoba and live there for thirty
days in order to show his obedience publicly. If he did all this,
the caliph would name him governor of Zaragoza. The Tujibi
also had to cut any relationship with the Christians and commit
himself to paying taxes. He was not to provide help to the
caliph's enemies, but he was obliged to fight against those
whom the caliph would fight, even if they were members of his
own family. His elder son and one of his brothers were kept as
hostages. If he fulfilled these conditions, Muhammad ibn
Hashim al-Tujibi was to be appointed governor of Zaragoza for
life and his right to name a successor was acknowledged. 'Abd
al-Rahman III entered Zaragoza on 21 November 937 and the
document of the "submission" of Zaragoza was solemnly sworn
in the mosque in the presence of a large number of witnesses.
The caliph ordered the walls to be destroyed, as he had done
previously in other conquered towns.

BETRAYAL: THE BATTLE OF
SIMANCAS-ALHANDEGA (939)

The caliph had been able momentarily to quell the rebellious-
ness of the Upper Frontier at the cost of acknowledging a high
degree of autonomy. But even this halfway victory was resented

by the people of the frontier, as they demonstrated shortly after the submission of Zaragoza.

Previous campaigns had been directed against the northeastern regions, but it was easier to keep Christian expansion at bay by the existence of well-established Muslim settlements in the Ebro valley. In 939 'Abd al-Rahman III moved against Leonese and Castilian territory, aiming at the town of Simancas, in an area where the Christians were pushing southwards into the Duero valley. He gathered a powerful army, both in men and equipment. In Toledo, his army was joined by troops of the Banu Dhi l-Nun, those of the lord of Huesca, Furtun ibn Muhammad (who would betray the caliph), and of the Tujibi lords of the Upper Frontier.

In August 939 the battle between Muslims and Christians in the area of Simancas produced uncertain results. There are different interpretations of the sequence and location of the military encounter. The crucial event was the ambushing by the Christians of 'Abd al-Rahman III's army; many were killed, and even the caliph's life was in great danger. He saved himself, but the Christians managed to take his coat of mail and his copy of the Qur'an. This defeat came to be known as that of al-Khandaq (the ditch or trench), apparently because the ambush took place in a ravine. But the name must have been used as a propaganda weapon against the caliph, as it referred to an episode from the early history of the Muslim community, when the Meccan Quraysh, before their conversion to Islam, under the leadership of Abu Sufyan (the ancestor of the Umayyads), attacked Medina and the Prophet ordered a trench (*khandaq*) to be dug, thus repelling the assailants. The defeat of another Umayyad, 'Abd al-Rahman III, was thus linked to that of his ancestor and therefore the name was probably used tauntingly against the caliph. Official documents tried hard to play down the defeat, insisting on the treacherous behavior on the part of some of the caliphal troops, who had allegedly helped the enemy by withdrawing from the battle.

Disaffection towards the Umayyads among the people of the frontier was not new, as they resented any attempts to reduce their autonomy, and make them pay taxes and participate in the campaigns organized from Cordoba. We have seen that in 917 some of the frontier people were described as religious hypocrites because their treacherous conduct helped the Christians defeat the Muslims. If weakening the caliph in order to strengthen their autonomy was the rationale for some of the frontier lords' behavior, the members of the caliphal army (*jund*) had their own grievances, the most important being the fact that command had been given to Najda ibn Husayn, a man who did not belong to the old Arab and client elites and whose appointment was therefore resented.

The defeat at Simancas coincided with a solar eclipse and was followed by a darkness that covered the sun for seven days. The defeat had wide-ranging and lasting consequences. Muhammad ibn Hashim al-Tujibi, lord of Zaragoza, was captured and his imprisonment in Leonese lands lasted for two years. Furtun ibn Muhammad, one of the traitors, was captured and crucified in Cordoba, as were ten members of the *jund* who had fled during the battle. One witness found their painful death so unbearable that he fainted. But their execution seems to have been a token gesture, because the rest of the participants went unpunished, an indication that the caliph was unable or unwilling to extend his reprisals beyond them. Until then, he had pursued a determined policy of extending his direct control over the frontier area, although he had to content himself momentarily with indirect control. The battle of Simancas revealed that the autonomy of the local lineages was there to last. In fact, from 939 onwards, military activity in the Upper Frontier was left in the hands of the local lords, who, as recorded by the chronicler Ibn Hayyan, had inherited their lands from their ancestors and given ample proof of their courage and ability in war. Each year, the caliph renewed their right to rule over their lands, sending them presents and giving them lavish receptions on their visits to Cordoba. The absence of serious rebellions during the rest of 'Abd al-Rahman III's reign and that of his successor has been taken to mean that the caliph and the local lineages had found an acceptable balance between central control and local autonomy.

Muhammad ibn Hashim al-Tujibi, who had been taken captive at Simancas, was later freed thanks to the caliph's intervention and returned to the Upper Frontier, where he fought against the king of Navarra and the count of Castille. He also fought against the Magyar (Hungarian) peoples who had reached the Iberian peninsula from the north in 942. In 950, he was succeeded as lord of Zaragoza by his son Yahya. Other members of the Tujibi family controlled different districts of the Upper Frontier.

A brother of Furtun ibn Muhammad, who had been executed as a traitor, ruled in Huesca, after having been in Cordoba in 940 to pledge obedience to the caliph. Internal conflicts appeared, however, within his lineage, perhaps motivated by difference of opinions regarding the alliance with the king of Navarra, with whom they had family links. Intermarriage between Christian and Muslim elites – a feature of frontier politics during the eighth and ninth centuries – was then becoming a thing of the past. Its end was an indication of the role that religion would play in the events of later centuries, particularly during the times of the Crusades and the militant *jihad* Berber movements.

The Berber Banu Dhi l-Nun, who in the eleventh century would take power as independent rulers of Toledo, continued to be active in the Middle Frontier, leading military expeditions against the Christians, especially in Castilian territory.

In those regions where the caliph's men were able to exert direct control, some took advantage of their position in the caliphal administration to acquire local power. Military commanders such as Ghalib, a freedman of the caliph, were destined to become important agents in the politics of the second half of the tenth century.

Simancas was the last battle of the caliph, who never took part in military campaigns again. Was it because he was afraid of another betrayal on the part of his army and thus of endangering his life again? Whatever the reason, the caliph who had fought thirteen campaigns in twenty years concentrated his efforts on the building of Madinat al-Zahra'.

RELATIONSHIPS WITH THE CHRISTIAN POLITIES

During the first three decades of his reign, 'Abd al-Rahman III's interventions in the frontier regions were always reactions to Navarran, Leonese, and Castilian activities. His aim was the defence and maintenance of his frontiers, without any attempt at increasing the territory under his rule in the Iberian peninsula. In fact, as we have seen in the previous chapters, Muslim campaigns usually took place after the Christians had advanced their positions or initiated military attacks, taking advantage of the fact that the Umayyad army was then mostly occupied fighting in the central lands of al-Andalus and that the frontier lords were involved in internal conflicts or willing to establish alliances with the Christians against Cordoban attempts to limit their autonomy. The people of Toledo, for example, are described as always willing to involve the Christians in their affairs, seeking their help against the Umayyads.

Especially worrying for the Muslims was Christian settlement on the left bank of the Duero river from the beginning of the tenth century. One of the most debated issues in Spanish historiography has been to what extent the Duero valley was a wasteland when it was repopulated by the Christians. In fact these lands were never depopulated. If the existing settlements have left few traces in the historical records this is because they were not part of any visible polity. The so-called repopulation of the Duero valley was partly the process by which existing populations increased their numbers by the arrival of emigrants from the north and the south (the Mozarabs), but mostly it reflects the emergence of new political and military frameworks of the activities of those populations. In 921, the Muslim troops who took part in the campaign against Osma remarked the presence in the area around Clunia of well-kept villages and extensive cultivated fields. In 930, a certain degree of unification among the different Castilian counts was achieved, a process of political convergence that is usually rendered as the birth of a new Christian polity, the county of Castille. Around that time, Simancas, the town attacked in 939, became a bishopric.

Christian expansion was checked after the 930s, owing both to Christian internal conflicts and to greater Muslim military investment. Frontal encounters with Christian armies seem to have been avoided and continuous harassment from different directions favored. There may also have been attempts at promoting a Muslim "repopulation" of the frontier, especially in the central area. Medinaceli became the new centre for Muslim military activity, facing the territory where Christian settlement and expansion had become especially dangerous. It was fortified in 946 by the freedman of the caliph, Ghalib, who was accompanied by a jurist of Berber origin, Muhammad ibn 'Abd Allah ibn Yahya ibn Abi 'Isa. Another jurist and also a Berber,

Mundhir ibn Sa'id al-Balluti (whom we shall encounter again), was active between 942 and 945 as judge of the frontier regions and responsible for any dealings with the Christians kingdoms. This presence of jurists acting on behalf of the caliph seems to point to an Umayyad policy more of conviction than confrontation with the Muslim population in the strategically crucial frontier area.

But if Christian expansion was checked, the campaigns organized almost every year by 'Abd al-Rahman III and the frontier lords against the Christian kingdoms did not lead to any actual recovery of land. Campaigns normally took place in spring and summer in order to ensure that the riding and pack animals could be fed, and also to prevent the enemy from harvesting their crops. The campaigns aimed at weakening the enemy to prevent attacks, and at obtaining captives and booty, not at reconquest. The inability to reverse the territorial losses had to do, on the Muslim side, with the tensions between Cordoban rule and local autonomy, with the fights within and among the local frontier lineages, and with the opening of a second frontier, that of North Africa, to which we shall come in a moment.

Diplomatic relationships went hand in hand with military activity. Treaties were signed and alliances established with the Christian kingdoms for a variety of reasons. During the caliphal campaign of 934 against the rebel lords of the Upper Frontier and the Christians, Queen Toda of Navarra established contact with 'Abd al-Rahman III, reminding him of their common Basque origins, offering him an alliance and asking him to acknowledge her son García Sánchez as king of Navarra, which the caliph did. In 958, Toda again contacted the caliph. Her grandson, the king of León, Sancho the Fat (r. 956–66), had been dethroned in 957 by some members of the nobility and sought refuge with her. They both traveled to Cordoba in an act

of submission and consequently Sancho resumed his reign in
960. He was also cured of his obesity – and thus able to mount
his horse with dignity – by a Jewish doctor, Hasday ibn Shaprut,
an official in caliphal government employ.

We have seen that in 935, the caliph had signed a treaty with
the king of León in order to ensure that Zaragoza could not
count on Christian help. In 940, the caliph sent Hasday ibn
Shaprut to León to obtain the freedom of Muhammad ibn
Hashim al-Tujibi, captured at the battle of Simancas. The Jewish
ambassador stayed for seven months in the Leonese capital,
where two bishops from al-Andalus also arrived to intercede
for al-Tujibi, whose freedom was finally obtained. The caliphal
copy of the Qur'an captured at Simancas was also recovered.
Shortly afterwards, a treaty was signed with Ramiro II that
brought peace from Santarén to Huesca, but which was short-
lived. Also in 940, Hasday ibn Shaprut was sent to Barcelona to
sign a treaty with the counts of the area and those of southern
France, who wanted to guarantee their commercial exchange
with al-Andalus. In 955 Ordoño III asked for peace, an indication of the weakness of the Christian kingdoms in relationship
to the Cordoban caliphate at the time. Hasday ibn Shaprut was
in charge of bringing to him the document with the conditions
imposed by 'Abd al-Rahman III.

But diplomatic relationships were not limited to the
Christian kingdoms of the Iberian peninsula. An embassy from
the island of Sardinia came to Cordoba asking for a peace treaty.
It was accompanied by Italian merchants from Amalfi, whose
goods were sold at a good price, and a fruitful commercial
exchange was started. Ambassadors came and went between
Germany and Byzantium.

In 953, the German king Otto I, who was crowned emperor
by the Pope shortly afterwards, sent the monk John of Gorze as
an emissary to Cordoba in order to protest against the damages

caused by Muslim pirates, especially those of Fraxinetum (Fraxinetum disappeared during the reign of al-Hakam II, r. 961–76). Otto's letters to the caliph were deemed to contain material offensive to the Prophet, and as a result John of Gorze was kept waiting in Cordoba for three years. An ambassador of the caliph was sent to Otto's court in order to have the letters replaced by more acceptable ones. This ambassador was a Christian, Recemund, later to be appointed bishop of Elvira (Granada), and he returned in 956, whereupon the unfortunate John of Gorze was finally able to present his case and go home.

In 955, the Fatimids attacked the port of Almería, plundering the shipyard and the city. This attack may have prompted 'Abd al-Rahman III to send an embassy with presents to Constantinople so as to win the emperor Constantine VII Porphyrogenitus over for a concerted effort against the Fatimids. But the plans to weaken the Fatimids through attacks on two fronts came to nothing as the Byzantines were busy on their eastern frontiers and decided to maintain their armistice with the Fatimids, to whom they paid tribute in exchange for not having their possessions in Lower Italy attacked.

Diplomatic relationships between the caliph and the Byzantine emperor had started earlier. In 948–9 (or perhaps earlier in 945–6), a Byzantine embassy arrived in al-Andalus, after almost a century without any relevant diplomatic contacts. No details are given about the specific reasons behind it, although Byzantine and Fatimid rivalry in the Mediterranean, especially in Lower Italy, made the contact with Byzantium's enemies advisable. The letter brought by the ambassador and addressed to the caliph by Constantine VII was written in gold on blue parchment and it was accompanied by two precious books. One was Dioscorides' pharmacological treatise written in Greek, which prompted the caliph to ask the emperor for a translator as he could not find anyone who read that language in al-Andalus. Three years later the monk Nicholas arrived in al-Andalus and worked with a team including Hasday ibn Shaprut. The other gift was the Latin text of Orosius' history (see below, p. 117). A Cordoban embassy was then sent in exchange to Constantinople, and the Christian Recemund took part in it.

Foreign embassies have always been important in narratives meant to emphasize the power of rulers and the splendor of their courts. The descriptions of how the Byzantine ambassadors were captivated by their ostentatious reception at the Cordoban court have certainly undergone a process of embellishment and adaptation to pre-existing conceptions. Material circulating about embassies to other Muslim rulers and related folk tales were adapted to fit 'Abd al-Rahman III's court. Thus, the famous mystic Ibn 'Arabi, writing in the twelfth century, records a legendary account of how Frankish ambassadors arrived at the caliph's court, describing their astonishment at its magnificence and wealth. In Madinat al-Zahra', they took the chamberlains, dressed with brocade and silk and seated on thrones, for the caliph, who to their surprise was instead dressed very poorly and sitting on the floor, having in front of him a Qur'an, a sword, and fire. The caliph explained to them that God had ordered the Muslims to invite the infidels to the Book of God and, if they refused, to the sword, in which case their destiny would be the fire. Filled with terror, the Christians signed a treaty, accepting all the caliph's conditions.

CONFLICT WITH THE FATIMIDS AND NORTH AFRICAN POLICIES

When the Prophet Muhammad died, the young Muslim community had to solve the problem of his succession and for three centuries there were many diverging views on the matter. The Muslims who came to be known as Sunnis were those who accepted the legitimacy of Abu Bakr, 'Umar, 'Uthman, and 'Ali, the first successors of the Prophet as rulers of the Islamic community, as well as the legitimacy of the Umayyads and 'Abbasids who ruled afterwards. For Sunnis, the caliph was the delegate of God's Prophet and although he was not denied religious competence, he shared responsibility with the scholars, the experts on religious knowledge, and its interpreters. Shi'is, on the contrary, believed that the head of the community should always be a member of the family of the Prophet, who partook of the charisma of Muhammad. The Shi'i imams were thus conceived as delegates of God on earth, enjoying infallibility and supernatural knowledge, and scholars, who in the Isma'ili Shi'i conception were missionaries or propagandists, were subordinate to them.

Shi'ism never found a congenial atmosphere in al-Andalus, thanks to the deep impact that the establishment of the Umayyad dynasty had on this province. The Umayyads were outspoken opponents of the Shi'is, as the rise of the first dynasty of Islam had happened precisely in opposition to 'Ali, the Prophet's cousin and son-in-law. The Umayyads had been overthrown by the 'Abbasids, who in the early stages of their accession to power had found support among Shi'i sympathizers because of their claim to support the rights of the Prophet's family. The Umayyads of al-Andalus did not forget their anti-Shi'i past. Andalusi Umayyad identity was forged as anti-Shi'i more than as Sunni.

North Africa did not share this deeply engrained Umayyad anti-Shi'ism. In the Maghreb, a descendant of the Prophet had founded the Idrisid dynasty. The Shi'ism of the Idrisids was limited to genealogical legitimacy and to occasional references to messianic expectations. But the Fatimids were something else. They presented themselves as descendants of the Prophet and claimed to be the true Shi'i (Isma'ili) imams with all their prerogatives and charismatic powers. We have seen how Isma'ili propagandists established their first base in 893 in what is now Algerian territory. There, missionary activity was successful among the Kutama Berbers, among whom a powerful army was raised. The Isma'ili imam, from his residence in Salamiya (Syria), traveled to North Africa escaping from his 'Abbasid persecutors, as the Umayyad 'Abd al-Rahman I and the first Idrisid imam had done before him. The Fatimids were thus replicating the foundation story of previous dynasties in the Islamic west. Having been able to overcome many dangers, the Isma'ili imam was proclaimed caliph in Qayrawan with the messianic title al-Mahdi in the year 910. The Fatimid dynasty ruled a vast extension of North African territory from Tunis until the year 973, when after the conquest of Egypt in 969 the Fatimid court moved to Cairo. Fatimid agents visited al-Andalus during the second half of the ninth century and their spies were still traveling in the Iberian peninsula during the time of 'Abd al-Rahman III. Two Fatimid missionaries brought Ibn Hafsun official robes, and the caliph al-Mahdi was named in the Friday sermon in the mosques of Hafsunid territory.

Fatimid propaganda claimed that the whole of the Islamic world would be conquered by the new caliphs, but it was not until 969 that they were able to conquer Egypt, which opened the road to Baghdad and enabled them to conquer the sacred cities of Mecca and Medina. Expansion proved easier towards the west, but there it involved conflict with the Umayyads, because what Andalusis referred to as "the other side (of the Straits of Gibraltar)" had close political and commercial links with al-Andalus and was seen as a strategic area for the defence and expansion of Umayyad rule. As Ibn Hafsun was receiving help from North Africa, in 914 'Abd al-Rahman III had his ships destroyed. At the same time, he promoted the development of the Umayyad fleet and of Algeciras, a strategic port for the control of the Straits of Gibraltar.

The first time the Fatimids encroached upon the Umayyad sphere of influence was in 917, when they attacked the North African town of Nakur, only one hundred and seventy kilometers distant from Málaga. Umayyad intervention on the other side of the Straits increased from then onwards. In 927, in the area surrounding Tetuan, the caliph is said to have fought against Hamim, a Berber prophet, whose activity should be understood as an offshoot of the messianic expectations heightened by the Fatimid experience. During the 920s and 930s, Umayyad armies captured several coastal ports such as Ceuta, which served as buffers against the Fatimids and provided termini for Andalusi exports and for the trans-Saharan gold and slave trade. But the Fatimids' power was also strong, as they had the control of Fez (conquered in 935) and the allegiance for many years of a branch of the Idrisids.

Together with military conquest, Umayyad policy in North Africa and especially in the Maghreb also contemplated allowing local Idrisid and Berber rulers to keep their privileges as long as they acknowledged the sovereignty of 'Abd al-Rahman III, whose adoption of the caliphal title was meant to counter the pull the Fatimid caliphate might have exercised among those rulers. Official robes and vast sums of money were used in fostering this aim. Andalusi Berber notables were chosen as ambassadors and delegates to deal with the North African allies. Letters were sent by the caliph in which the Umayyad boasted of his revival of religion and his fight against innovations, his plans for re-conquering the Islamic central lands, especially the holy city of Mecca, desecrated by the Karmatis, and his right to the caliphate of his ancestors, to whom the Berbers owed their conversion to Islam.

As the Umayyads and Fatimids fought for both direct and indirect control of the Maghreb, Berber ethnic divisions, especially that between Sanhaja and Zanata, gave expression to the alliances being then formed. The Zanata sided mostly with the Umayyads. The Sanhaja sided with the Fatimids, and when the Fatimid caliph al-Mu'izz (r. 953–75) left for Egypt, the Sanhaja Zirids were left as his representatives in North Africa. The Umayyads were also approached by North African rebels against the Fatimids, the most important being Abu Yazid, the "Man of the Donkey." This Berber leader was a Khariji, a member of a militant Islamic sect considered heretical by Sunnis. But North African Sunnis, mostly Malikis, were willing to support him if that meant the end of Fatimid rule. And Abu Yazid with his army of Zanata Berbers almost succeeded in bringing about the fall of the Isma'ili dynasty. In 944 he conquered Tunis and Qayrawan, but he was unable to take Mahdiyya, the impregnable fortress by the sea built as a refuge in case of troubles by the first Fatimid caliph. A delegation of notables from Qayrawan was sent to Cordoba, and Abu Yazid's son Ayyub also traveled there formally to acknowledge the Umayyad caliph and seek Umayyad help (we have here the counterpart of what Ibn Hafsun had done when he acknowledged the Fatimid caliph against the Umayyads). But help arrived too late. In 946, the Umayyad navy sailed from Almería to support the "Man of the Donkey," but by the time they reached the North African coast Abu Yazid had been defeated and killed.

In fact, direct military confrontation between Umayyads and Fatimids was exceptional, as theirs was mostly a war waged through North African intermediaries. The latter were willing to act in that capacity because, on the one hand, they obtained material support and on the other hand, they could appear as caliphal agents, thus reinforcing their leadership within their tribal groups. There was therefore a convergence of interests: the caliph (be it Umayyad or Fatimid) gave legitimacy to the political aspirations of the Zanata or Sanhaja leaders and the latter acted as caliphal representatives, thereby extending caliphal authority.

By the 950s the battle for the Maghreb seemed to be favorable to the Umayyads. Some Idrisids and former allies of the Fatimids changed their allegiance. One of them was Ahmad ibn Abi Bakr al-Zanati, governor of Fez for the Fatimids, who in 955 ordered the cursing of the Shi'i imams from the pulpits and acknowledged the Umayyad caliph. 'Abd al-Rahman III transferred to him the fifth of the booty from his military campaigns against the Christians and with this money al-Zanati built the expanded prayer hall and minaret of the Qarawiyyin mosque in Fez in the name of the caliph of Cordoba. In the same year, as already mentioned, the port of Almería was attacked by the Fatimids, their first and only direct attack against Andalusi territory. In the spring a powerful Andalusi fleet, commanded by the freedman Ghalib, did some damage to the Fatimids in the Tunisian coast, but failed to conquer Mahdiyya. Shortly afterwards, al-Mu'izz put his freedman Jawhar in command of an army sent to subjugate the Maghreb, which he did between the years 958–60. Recovery of what had been lost in North Africa would be achieved by 'Abd al-Rahman III's successor, al-Hakam II, during whose reign the departure of the Fatimids for Egypt took place.

5

THE CALIPH'S FAMILY
AND HIS MEN

An imam of justice who wears
two crowns of authority and liberality.

Ibn 'Abd Rabbihi (transl. Salma Kh. Jayyusi)

THE CALIPH'S FAMILY

The eleventh-century Ibn Hazm criticized 'Abd al-Rahman III for having expelled from his royal palace one of his aunts, a half-sister of Mutarrif, the murderer of the caliph's father. Official historians, on the contrary, state that 'Abd al-Rahman III took care of her, as if the picture that the emir wanted to preserve for posterity was that of a united family that forgave and forgot internal misdemeanors and crimes.

'Abd al-Rahman III married the sister of Najda ibn Husayn, whom we have encountered as the military commander who did not belong to either the old Arab families or the client elite and whose appointment, resented by the latter, contributed to the betrayal of Simancas. Both sister and brother were of humble origin. We are not told what Najda did for a living before he entered the caliph's service, but the caliph is said to have met his sister near a river while she was working as a bleacher. The sources do not record her name, only that she became known as Umm Quraysh, "the mother of Qurashi men", Quraysh being the caliph's tribe. His marriage to her may have been the reason that her brother Najda had a successful career in the caliphal administration. Governor of Takurunna in 931 and later of Osuna, Najda was appointed director of the stable in 933, taking part in numerous campaigns, among them that of Osma in 934, when he was charged with ensuring forage for the mounts, accomplishing the mission to the caliph's satisfaction. He subsequently became an army commander, leading the cavalry against Pamplona after the submission of Zaragoza in 937. He was dismissed in 939–40 after the defeat at Simancas, and in 942 was appointed prefect of the higher police.

'Abd al-Rahman III also had a wife of a more conventional character. She was the daughter of his grandfather's brother, the emir al-Mundhir (r. 886–8), and called Fatima al-Qurashiyya. She had been educated in the royal palace under the emir 'Abd Allah's tutorship, so that they had probably grown up together. Fatima's noble lineage (she may have been a Qurashi not only on the paternal, but also on the maternal side) is reflected in the title "the Great Lady" given to her. It may have been a political marriage in order to avoid opposition from the descendants of the emir al-Mundhir, but endogamy was a usual practice among the Umayyads. They also took women from outside their lineage (whose children were Qurashis regardless of the mother's origins), but avoided giving away their own women. This marriage may have had another aspect. Her name, Fatima, was the name of the Prophet's daughter, the wife of Ali; she was a free woman, and the children she bore to the emir could boast a nobler lineage than that of children born of slave mothers or free women of humble origin such as Najda's sister. One of her sons, al-Mundhir, was referred to as Ibn al-Qurashiyya, "the son of the Qurashi woman" and we have already seen how exceptional it was for cognate links to be recorded. The second Fatimid caliph, al-Qa'im, was born of al-Mahdi's marriage to a paternal cousin, and was thus a Qurashi on both sides. Lineage was one of the areas of rivalry between the Umayyads and the Fatimids.

But in spite of his noble lineage, Fatima's son al-Mundhir did not inherit the caliphate. Fatima lost 'Abd al-Rahman III's favor because of the trick played against her by another of his wives, Marjan. This woman, a Christian slave, is described as beautiful, refined, elegant, sweet, and very clever. As already mentioned, a Muslim man can have four legal wives and an unlimited number of slave concubines. One day when the emir had decided to spend the night with Fatima, Marjan told Fatima that she would like to buy that night from her and offered a large sum of money. Fatima agreed and signed a document recording the sale. 'Abd al-Rahman spent the night with Marjan, who showed him the document signed by Fatima; thereafter he refused to visit her, and for all her high lineage her status was greatly diminished. By contrast, Marjan became the favorite of the emir, who rewarded her lavishly. Part of that money she spent on pious works, such as the construction of a mosque supported by an endowment, a common practice among royal women. Marjan was the mother of two daughters and three sons. One of them was al-Hakam, who inherited the caliphate. Having given birth, the slave Marjan became "the mother of a son" (*umm walad*), a status involving her manumission.

Another slave, Mushtaq, became the favourite during the last years of the caliph's life. She was the mother of the youngest and dearest of his sons, al-Mughira, who many years after his father's death was killed by some high officials of the dynasty (among them the future *de facto* ruler al-Mansur ibn Abi 'Amir) in order to eliminate a possible rival to their candidate to the throne, 'Abd al-Rahman's III grandson Hisham II.

Sexual intimacy with 'Abd al-Rahman III could bring lavish reward to his slave concubines, but also death. An anonymous slave with whom the caliph was enjoying himself in the gardens of Madinat al-Zahra' dared to show her displeasure at being kissed by him. Enraged, he called his eunuchs and ordered them to burn her face with a candle. On another occasion, when the caliph was in his villa of al-Na'ura (the waterwheel), the executioner was called into a room, where the eunuchs were holding a beautiful young woman who was begging for mercy, while the caliph insulted her. He ordered the executioner to behead the woman, which he did when his attempt to dissuade the caliph failed. Later on, the executioner found in his leather mat pearls and precious stones, which had obviously fallen from a necklace when her head was cut. He wanted to return them to the caliph, but 'Abd al-Rahman III told him to keep them, and in this way the executioner had money enough to buy a house.

'Abd al-Rahman III had sixteen daughters and eighteen or nineteen sons. Of the latter only eleven or twelve survived him. The male children were provided with an education in accordance to their natural capacities. 'Abd al-Rahman III followed with them the same policy as his great-grandfather, the emir Muhammad, who did not allow his male descendants to live in the royal palace. As they reached puberty, they were given palaces and lands, the rents of which, together with monthly stipends and an annual sum of money, wisely administered by a supervisor, sufficed to ensure a comfortable living. Their mothers chose their wives among women whom they had raised themselves. In the year 943, all the caliph's sons were living independently, except for al-Hakam, the heir to the throne. Having the adult male sons removed from the royal

palace of Cordoba was meant to diminish the possibility of conspiracies within the family. This practice contrasts to that of the
Fatimids, who kept princes ineligible for the succession as prisoners in the royal palace. 'Abd al-Rahman III also had many
grandsons, for some of whom he organized a celebration of
their circumcision in Madinat al-Zahra'.

The caliph-to-be al-Hakam was born in 915. In 921, when
he was only six years old and 'Abd al-Rahman III was away leading a campaign, al-Hakam was left as his representative in
Cordoba. From that year onwards, 'Abd al-Rahman III appears
to have made it clear that his son al-Hakam was destined to
inherit his position. He took him on some of his campaigns and
even put him in command of some of the troops at the age of
twelve, thus gradually incorporating his son into the running of
state affairs, while al-Hakam also devoted his time to study and
the promotion of knowledge, for which he is mostly known.

Al-Hakam's political and military training went together
with a very strict supervision of his private life. Al-Hakam was
not allowed to take any wife until very late in his life, and
rumors circulated about his love for young men. His lack of
male descendants became a pressing problem when he succeeded his father in 961 at the age of forty-six without an heir
(the future caliph Hisham II was born in 965). We are not told
the reasons for this extreme control on the part of 'Abd
al-Rahman III. Was it related to what his grandfather had done
with him? With the experience of two of his adult male sons
conspiring against him, the emir 'Abd Allah's choice of his
young orphan grandchild as his heir was probably intended as a
way to avoid any possibility of conspiracy on his part, while
having him under his strict supervision was meant to deter
others from using him. But al-Hakam was to grow into adult-
hood when the ruling emir was still young. His sexuality and
maturity, however, could be, and were, controlled.

'Abd al-Rahman III also followed in his grandfather's steps
by bringing about the death of one of his sons, 'Abd Allah,
whom he suspected of conspiracy, in 950 or 951. 'Abd Allah's
throat was cut by the caliph himself, according to one source,
during the Festival of the Sacrifice on the open-air oratory
where Muslims were slaughtering animals for the ritual sacrifice. The caliph thus took the role of the Prophet Abraham who
was ordered by God to slaughter his son (whether he was Isaac
or Isma'il is debated in the Islamic tradition). 'Abd Allah is said
to have criticized his father for his cruelty and his shedding of
blood. He, like his brother al-Hakam, was interested in the pur-
suit of knowledge, although he favored the Shafi'i legal school
whereas al-Hakam was a Maliki. Ibn Hazm praises 'Abd Allah
as a pious and virtuous man whom it was wrong for the caliph
to kill.

Conspiracies within the family were a real threat. Earlier in
his reign, in 921, 'Abd al-Rahman III had faced a conspiracy on
the part of his paternal uncle al-'Asi and his cousin Muhammad
ibn 'Abd al-Jabbar, who were executed that same year. In 936 a
member of the Umayyad family, Ahmad ibn Ishaq al-Qurashi,
was also executed, as we have seen. Even so, considering its
large numbers, the Umayyad family remained remarkably
united behind 'Abd al-Rahman III.

MEN OF THE SWORD AND MEN OF THE PEN

A closely-knit weft of tradition, loyalty, service, and reward
bound the caliph and his elites. The names that identified them
are recurrent in the sources. The Banu Abi 'Abda, the Banu
Jahwar, the Banu Hudayr, the Banu Futays, the Banu Shuhayd,
and others were linked to the Umayyads by ties of clientage
often dating from the time of the Umayyad caliphs of

Damascus. Other families, such as the Banu Zajjali, Banu Ilyas, or the Banu Ya'la were of Berber origin and their links with the Umayyads had been established in the Iberian peninsula, often with the aim of counteracting or frustrating the influence of the eastern Umayyad clients.

A distinctive feature of 'Abd al-Rahman III's form of government was the high mobility in official posts which makes extremely difficult any attempt at keeping track of the many appointments and dismissals of 'Abd al-Rahman III's men. Most of them belonged to client families. If in some cases the dismissals were motivated by dishonest behavior or misdemeanors (as in the case of the officials responsible for the minting of coins), in others it seems to have been just a way of ensuring that no one was in charge long enough to become troublesome and to make it clear that absolute (and arbitrary) power was in the hands of the ruler. Mobility also had the function of ensuring that all the caliph's men got their share of the resources administered by the state. Thus the same man or members of the same family would perform through the years as military commanders, governors, secretaries, supervisors of the tax collection, chiefs of police, and inspectors. Many were viziers during their careers, the vizierate being mostly an honorific post, as we shall see.

In exchange for obedience and service, the caliph would offer human kindness, not just monetary rewards. When 'Abbas, son of the vizier and commander Ibn Abi 'Abda, died in 915, 'Abd al-Rahman III offered his condolences and attended his funeral, appointing the deceased's brother 'Abdallah as chief of the higher police. In 927 Muhammad ibn Ahmad ibn Muhammad ibn Sa'id ibn Musa ibn Hudayr died at a young age, after having served the emir in different capacities. His death was a source of great grief to his father and his uncle, who was then chamberlain, and the caliph reacted by granting an official position to his younger brother, Musa, who had not even reached puberty, "in order to soothe the pain of their loss and to keep his memory alive."

In addition to the old families who specialized in serving the Umayyads, there were also new men who rose on the basis of personal links with him, and whose families benefited from those links. We have already met an example in Najda, the brother of one of his wives. The Banu Badr ibn Ahmad are another example. Badr ibn Ahmad was a foundling, whom the emir 'Abd Allah put into the service of his grandson. Having become his client, Badr played a crucial role in the early period of 'Abd al-Rahman III's reign as a trusted military commander in charge of the first military campaigns and as the first chamberlain of the emir. His sons were favored with positions mostly in the civil administration, for example, as governors of Seville, surely as a way to counteract the Arab predominance in the region.

The traditional *jund* was maintained in the pre-Simancas years, although the caliph had already started changes aiming at diminishing the autonomy of the military tribal groups. After Simancas, the caliph's policy was to increase the number of the professional or mercenary troops with men of diverse provenance. Former rebels, among them even Christians, were inscribed on the payroll. North African mercenary troops, especially from Tangiers, which had been already employed by the emir 'Abd Allah, were active in some campaigns of 'Abd al-Rahman III. The Berbers would become especially important in al-Hakam II's army, in a process contributing to the dismantling of the caliphate in the so-called "Berber anarchy" at the end of the tenth century. Slaves formed the personal guard of the caliph.

An important military achievement of 'Abd al-Rahman III was the building of a powerful navy. On the sea, the Fatimid threat had added to the Viking danger. Almería became the

most important Umayyad port and the production of its shipyard increased. The expertise of its sailors in maritime traffic
and commercial shipping must have been decisive in the
remarkable development achieved by the naval forces, thanks
to which the Umayyads could pursue a maritime policy in the
Mediterranean. The integration of the Balearic Islands into the
Umayyad state was related to this development, as shown by
the appointment of governors and judges there from 930
onwards. Naval expeditions departing from Almería in 935 and
943 were directed towards the Frankish coasts.

Client families such as the Banu Shuhayd, Banu l-Zajjali,
Banu Jahwar, and Banu Futays supplied many secretaries to the
caliphal chancery. Secretaries were men of letters whose training involved calligraphy and knowledge of Arabic belles lettres.
There were two basic chancery functions. The most prestigious
was dealing with the official correspondence, some examples
of which have been preserved by the historian Ibn Hayyan: the
letter proclaiming the caliphal title of 'Abd al-Rahman III, a
letter to be read in the mosques informing of the battle of
Simancas, as well as letters exchanged with the North African
allies. The other function of the chancery was the administration of public finances, based on meticulous tax-collection,
carried out by "men of numbers" rather than by men of letters.

All this involved an extensive bureaucracy. In 955, the caliph
undertook an administrative reform consisting in the creation
of four bureaus directed by viziers. One bureau dealt with the
inter-administrative correspondence; the second with that of
the frontier regions; the third, with the transmission of orders
and decrees; the fourth dealt with the supervision of complaints and the affairs of subjects. This reform took place in
the same year that the Fatimids attacked the port of Almería,
causing severe destruction. If the attack was seen as the prelude
to a large-scale Fatimid intervention, this may have prompted

the caliph to strengthen the control of the territory under his rule.

The vizierate was not always a position involving the supervision or direction of a specific bureau in the administration. More commonly, it was a mere dignity, an honorific title signaling that the person bearing it enjoyed a high position in the political and social hierarchy, and was entitled to a monetary payment. Not only civil functionaries but also military chiefs could be named viziers. Their main role was as advisors to the ruler, who consulted them regularly. Together with the members of the royal family, the viziers were the first to swear allegiance to the new ruler.

Rebels who returned to obedience were sometimes appointed as viziers. This was the case of the Sevillan Muhammad ibn Ibrahim ibn Hajjaj in 913–14, although he only performed in the office for one day, as 'Abd al-Rahman III suspected him of treason and sent him to prison, where he died in 914–15. In 941, when Muhammad ibn Hashim al-Tujibi was freed by Ramiro II and arrived in Cordoba, he was made vizier, joining the other viziers in their meeting hall until he was sent back to Zaragoza as military commander.

As indicated, the conspiracy of the Umayyads al-Asi and Muhammad ibn 'Abd al-Jabbar took place in 921, and in that same year the trusted chamberlain Badr ibn Ahmad died. It was after this date, between 922 and 934, that the official chronicles start recording an increasing number of appointments and dismissals of viziers, ranging from six to ten per year. Between 934 and 942 there was a minimum of nine viziers per year. In 939, 'Abd al-Malik ibn Shuhayd was appointed to the higher police and to the supervision of complaints, as well as to the "double vizierate" (*dhu l-wizaratayn*), a higher honorific title that he obtained after having offered costly presents to the caliph, but which also allowed him to gain vast sums of money.

The reasons for this appointment are not clear: perhaps the caliph was in need of money or perhaps Ibn Shuhayd helped him to calm the unrest provoked by the betrayal of Simancas in that same year.

The number of viziers increased to sixteen in 942, a number never witnessed before, as it is remarked in the chronicles. This high number may point to dissatisfaction among the Umayyad elites, perhaps in connection with the fact that the "new man" Najda ibn Husayn was named chief of the higher police in that year, or perhaps related to the large sums paid to 'Abd al-Malik ibn Shuhayd in his position of the "double vizierate". Either way, the caliph would have tried to appease them by granting them salaried dignities, and it is perhaps not accidental that Ibn Shuhayd was dismissed in the same year, officially because a man in charge of the minting of coins, who was under his supervision, was found guilty of fraud.

In the east there was usually only one vizier, who was the main auxiliary of the ruler, transmitting and carrying out his order and sometimes even making decisions in his name. There was a similar position in al-Andalus, but it was occupied by the chamberlain (*hajib*), not by a vizier. The chamberlain was first and foremost in charge of the ruler's home, but he also acted as the representative of the ruler in political, diplomatic, and military activities and was charged with the highest administrative responsibilities in the state. 'Abd al-Rahman III's first *hajib* was his client Badr ibn Ahmad. After his death in 921, Musa ibn Muhammad ibn Sa'id ibn Musa ibn Hudayr was named *hajib*. When he died in 932, the position remained vacant for the rest of 'Abd al-Rahman III's reign. The freshly proclaimed caliph may not have found someone he trusted, and perhaps by then he felt experienced enough to manage the state all by himself. He may have wanted to imitate the Fatimid caliph, who did not appoint any vizier (in the eastern sense of the term), regarding it as unfitting to a Shi'i imam. Or 'Abd al-Rahman III may have foreseen the danger inherent in relying so much on a single man, who might end up by taking over. That was in fact what happened when al-Mansur ibn Abi 'Amir became the *hajib* of 'Abd al-Rahman III's grandson.

SLAVES AND EUNUCHS

The fact that the emir 'Abd Allah had chosen him as his heir did not mean that 'Abd al-Rahman III was pampered by his grandfather. The emir 'Abd Allah was famously stingy, probably because of the drastic reduction in taxation caused by the state of rebellion in most of his lands. One day when the young 'Abd al-Rahman was riding with the emir 'Abd Allah, they stopped for prayer and 'Abd al-Rahman's horse fled. 'Abd Allah was surprised that his grandson was not accompanied by a servant eunuch who would hold his horse. 'Abd al-Rahman's answer was that he did not have enough money to buy that kind of servant. Later his grandfather gave him a halter covered with silk to tie up the horse. A eunuch would have been better of course, but they were much too expensive.

According to Ibn Hawqal, slaves were castrated in al-Andalus by Jews and exported from there to the rest of the Islamic world. According to other sources, eunuchs were also "manufactured" at Verdun (France), where the merchants, both Jewish and non-Jewish, grew rich from their trade. Wherever they came from, eunuchs played an important role in the personal service of the ruler, especially as guards of the female members of his family. The story of how Marjan's trickery ousted Fatima al-Qurashiyya from 'Abd al-Rahman III's favor was recorded in a historical chronicle because it was narrated by Talal, a court eunuch who worked as secretary. The barber and cupper of 'Abd al-Rahman III was also a eunuch, called Fath.

Eunuchs could also be employed as military commanders, as in the case of Ibrahim, who took part in the conquest of Santarén in 939 and was responsible for bringing Furtun ibn Muhammad, the traitor of Simancas, to Cordoba; or in the case of Badr, referred to as "master of the sword", who was sent with troops to Ceuta in 960. Two eunuchs, Tammam and Yasir, were in charge of receiving the Byzantine ambassador in 949.

Some eunuchs were of Saqaliba origin. The term Saqaliba, which strictly speaking meant slaves of Slavonic origin, seems to have been applied to slaves of European provenance in general, so in effect it meant white slaves. Merchants brought them from the Slav regions via Central Europe to al-Andalus, and from there some were exported to the rest of the Islamic world, being highly valued at the rulers' courts. The most famous of 'Abd al-Rahman III's Saqaliba was Ja'far al-Saqlabi, a eunuch who was manumitted in 959–60, shortly before the caliph's death. This Ja'far was close to al-Hakam II, whom he served as chamberlain, secretary, and head of the manufacture of royal clothes before his death in 970–1; his name even appeared on coins. The number of Saqaliba court officials increased dramatically during the reign of al-Hakam II and later under al-Mansur ibn Abi 'Amir. After the fall of the caliphate some of them were able to establish their own kingdoms.

Slaves had been employed in the Umayyad army from an early date and they were also used by 'Abd al-Rahman III. For example, in the campaign of Seville of 913 the chamberlain Badr ibn Ahmad was accompanied by thirty slaves, referred to as "mutes", as they did not speak Arabic. Slaves of unknown origin held important positions. Durri was named chief of police in

925 and commanded troops in different caliphal campaigns. Qand was put in charge of military equipment and ownerless inheritances and in 947 led an expedition from Toledo. Five prisoners of war taken from the Magyars who had invaded al-Andalus from the north were sent to Cordoba (they wore their original attire and must have caused great curiosity). They eventually converted to Islam and became pages of the caliph. As mentioned before, slaves formed the personal guard of the caliph, having the advantage that they belonged to the caliph in person and were devoted only to him. Carried off in child-hood, with no family connections, they were entirely depend-ent on their master, who remained their patron if they were manumitted.

The most famous slave was Ghalib ibn 'Abd al-Rahman, whose patronymic announced that he was like "a son" of the caliph, who had manumitted him. Ghalib commanded many military campaigns both on the frontiers of al-Andalus and in North Africa from 942 onwards. He also served 'Abd al-Rahman III's successors, who granted him the honorific titles of "the two swords" and "the two vizierates." Ghalib's daughter Asma' married al-Mansur ibn Abi 'Amir in 977, when the latter was trying to enhance his position and take over from the powerful chamberlain Ja'far al-Mushafi. Al-Mansur ibn Abi 'Amir would eventually be responsible for Ghalib's death.

The Fatimids, who had gained their caliphate with the help of a Berber army, soon employed slaves and Saqaliba as military commanders in order to reduce the influence of the Berbers. Jawhar, a Christian slave whose origins are debated, was the conqueror of Egypt. The eunuch Maysur led many campaigns in the Maghreb. Maysur is referred to as "castrated cockerel" and similar epithets in the letters sent to 'Abd al-Rahman III by his North African allies. We can only imagine the feelings of the eunuch secretaries of the Umayyad caliph when they read such crude descriptions of their Fatimid counterparts.

HIERARCHIES AND EGALITARIANISM AMONG THE MUSLIM POPULATION

Once mere *primi inter pares* among the Muslim Arabs, the Umayyad emirs had progressively separated themselves from their subjects. In 865 Muhammad I (the great-grandfather of 'Abd al-Rahman III) had ordered an enclosure (*maqsura*) to be built in the great mosque of Cordoba, a protected space that separated the emir and his close attendants from the rest of the believers during prayer. Later on, the emir 'Abd Allah connected the *maqsura* directly with the palace through a covered passage (see above, p. 35). Entry into the *maqsura* was a mark of privilege: when the Cordoban scholar and Umayyad client, Ja'far ibn Yahya ibn Ibrahim ibn Muzayn (d. 903–4), was not allowed to pray there, his pain at his exclusion was followed by his death. This separation among believers happened in the mosque, a religious space that was supposed to be egalitarian. Needless to say, the palace had always allowed far more limited access to the ruler. That access became increasingly more hierarchical with 'Abd al-Rahman III and his successors, as evidenced by descriptions of caliphal receptions. Although the Cordoban Umayyads did not produce any "Book of ceremonies" such as those written for the 'Abbasids or the Byzantines, the chronicles offer information on the elaborate ceremonial which had developed in court receptions for foreign delegations and during religious festivals under al-Hakam II.

The caliph al-Hakam II would appear in court ceremonies in the reception halls of his palaces surrounded by his immediate family, emphasizing the importance of the Umayyad lineage. Quraysh, the caliph's tribe, and his clients, were positioned to the left of the caliph. In front of him were aligned high-ranking officials: the viziers, followed by the prefects of the higher and middle police, the functionaries of the treasury, the administrators of the army, and the secretaries. Slaves and eunuch servants were probably placed behind the high-ranking officials, whereas files of regular troops were placed outside the palace hall. Magistrates, rural district judges, jurists, official witnesses, and notables of Cordoba were among those waiting outside the hall, also in order.

This ceremonial probably derived from rules already established in 'Abd al-Rahman III's time, but we have little information about official receptions during his reign. The pact formalizing the submission of Muhammad ibn Hashim al-Tujibi of Zaragoza gives us a very similar picture of the elites surrounding the caliph: high ranking officials, both civil and religious, members of the caliph's immediate family, and relatives from the Quraysh tribe.

Only a few Umayyads and Qurashis are recorded as having had official positions in the caliphal administration. As stated above, those families who had an almost patrimonial monopoly on government offices were mostly Umayyad clients (*mawali*). Some of them were the descendants of the Umayyad *mawali* who had formed part of the Muslim armies settled in the Iberian peninsula and who had supported the cause of the first Umayyad emir. Others were new clients (some Berbers, some from the local population), with links established either by manumission or contractual clientage with 'Abd al-Rahman I and his successors.

By the tenth century, the term *mawali*, in the plural, was used almost exclusively to refer to what appears to be an institutionalized social group formed by those who were loyal to the ruling Umayyad family, and meaning the opposite of "Arabs", which is often a synonym for rebels. The Umayyads took care not to be referred to as "Arabs" and in Umayyad chronicles the Arabs or Arab clients employed in the caliphal administration were not usually referred to by their tribal *nisbas*. In fact, the Umayyads, and especially 'Abd al-Rahman III, tried to distance themselves from the Arabs and regarded Qurayshis and the Umayyad family as in a category apart from the rest of the Arabs. Having to rule an ethnically diverse population, the caliph was thus trying not to be associated with a particular ethnic group, so as to build for himself a wider support basis.

The Arabs, like the Berbers and the Muwallads, had rebelled against Umayyad rule. 'Abd al-Rahman III did not trust them and in fact he did what he could to undermine their power: he appointed non-Arabs as governors of the *jund* districts and gave other important military positions to non-Arabs. But Arab (and Berber) power was not wiped out as Muwallad power was. No Muwallad ruler was allowed to remain in his local power base, whereas Arabs and Berbers were. After the collapse of the caliphate, Arab and Berber Party kingdoms were established, but we do not find any Muwallad political entities.

The idea of Arab supremacy was difficult to eradicate in a society where memory of Arab ancestry was still recorded and cherished, and where the ruler's claim to legitimacy rested on membership of an Arab tribe, even if this claim was filtered through the religious merits of the Quraysh, the tribe of the Prophet. The sheer fact that religious merit and Arab identity were so hard to separate did not help (the Prophet had himself been an Arab, the Qur'an was in Arabic, the annual pilgrimage was to a sanctuary in Arabia, and love of the Arabs was widely regarded as part of the faith). One example suffices to show that, for all his mistrust of the Arabs, 'Abd al-Rahman III could not escape his own background or the social importance Arabs still retained. The Banu Adha al-Hamdani kept their local power after their submission. A member of this Arab family, Ahmad ibn Muhammad ibn Adha, is described as good looking, generous, eloquent, and cultivated. He attracted the caliph's attention and obtained many benefits and an elevated position from him. This Ahmad ibn Muhammad ibn Adha delivered a renowned speech praising 'Abd al-Rahman III as a descendant of the Prophet (which the caliph was not in the way the Fatimid imam was) and as a righteous imam through whom the Arabs increased their splendor and brilliance: the Prophet and Arab power are closely entwined here. When this Ahmad was governor of Jaén, the caliph sent him a high-ranking non-Arab official (probably a slave), named al-Qalafat, to check his performance in a certain matter. Ibn Adha found al-Qalafat's control unbearable and his behavior insolent and rude, and gave orders to have him flogged with a hundred lashes. Al-Qalafat managed to flee and complained to the caliph. 'Abd al-Rahman III is said to have contemplated punishing Ibn Adha, but he was dissuaded by his vizier 'Abd al-Malik ibn Jahwar (a friend of Ibn Adha), who improvised some verses in which al-Qalafat's trial was ridiculed. The caliph laughed and Ibn Adha went unpunished. Al-Qalafat would never have dared to act with Ibn Adha as Ibn Adha had with him (unless obeying the caliph's orders). Being an Arab in the tenth century still entailed privilege, pride, and authority.

Berbers among the urban elites or the caliph's *mawali* do not seem to have suffered discrimination, although their origins could be mentioned in abusive terms by Arabs and by those *mawali* whose clientage had been established by the Umayyads in the east and who took pride in their old ties with the dynasty. The memory of those origins was not lost, as shown by the fact that Berber scholars and officials were often employed in missions dealing with Berber elements in both al-Andalus and North Africa.

During the campaign of 913, a follower of Ibn Hafsun dared to insult the emir. A man in charge of the mules in the emir's army retorted that 'Abd al-Rahman III would not leave without Ibn Hafsun's head. Having heard this, the emir ordered that he should be enrolled in the cavalry and gave him a horse and money. This man thus saw his social position elevated. Whether true or not, this anecdote had an egalitarian message and as such it was circulated.

The Muslim tradition of egalitarianism found its way in al-Andalus with the introduction of Arabo-Islamic classical literature in Umayyad court circles, such as the literary compilation by Ibn 'Abd Rabbihi (d. 940). The Umayyad caliphs in fact promoted the creation of an Andalusi identity that revolved around the Islamic religion and Arab culture, while trying to relegate Arabic ethnicity to a secondary position. The main influence on this common Andalusi identity came from the incorporation of converts in the world of Muslim scholarship.

By the tenth century, the experts on religious knowledge, the *'ulama*, were mostly of convert origin, as shown by the absence of any tribal affiliation in their names. Ahmad ibn Baqi ibn Makhlad was appointed judge of Cordoba by 'Abd al-Rahman III. Asked about his family's origins, he answered that they were descendants of a client (*mawla*) of a woman from Jaén. His honesty was considered remarkable: had he claimed Arab origins nobody would have dared to deny it. This anecdote points to a discernable trend during the caliphate of 'Abd al-Rahman III of establishing a Muslim's social standing on the basis either of his service to the caliph or of his religious merits, not his ethnic origin.

At the same time, the last judge of 'Abd al-Rahman III and the first of al-Hakam II, the Berber Mundhir ibn Sa'id al-Balluti (d. 966), is said to have promoted the adoption of the *nisba* al-Ansari by those who had no Arab tribal affiliation. This *nisba*

derived from the name Ansar ("Helpers") given to Arab tribesmen in Medina who had helped the Prophet when he settled
there. Mundhir is recorded as saying that whoever helped
the Prophet (i.e., the Islamic religion), at whatever time, was
entitled to be called an Ansari. He was thus facilitating the
use of a *nisba* with a purely religious meaning, a step which
would have important influence in the history of al-Andalus.
Some Andalusis who had no Arab genealogy adopted this
nisba, thus signalling their commitment to Islam. In the new
caliphal society, to be a Muslim was what mattered, even if in
practice Arabs still retained a special status for all the reasons
given above.

CHRISTIANS AND JEWS

If being a Muslim was what mattered most, what about
Christians and Jews? They were entitled to certain rights in
al-Andalus, as elsewhere in the Islamic world. They were free to
practice their religion, although they were obliged to keep a low
profile in their external ritual manifestations, and they were
free to be judged by their own laws, except when Muslims were
also involved, in which case Islamic law prevailed. Several
restrictions applied to Christians and Jews in contrast to their
fellow Muslims. This discriminatory tolerance was the *dhimma*
pact granted to Christians, Jews, and other non-Muslims who
lived in Muslim territory, where they constituted "protected
groups" or legitimate religious communities. Even as *dhimmis*,
their rejection of Muhammad's prophecy made them unbelievers, like those living outside Muslim territory. *Dhimmis*
could be fought if they were thought to be crossing the boundaries of their subordinate status, and of course also if they
rebelled.

THE CALIPH'S FAMILY AND HIS MEN **99**

Christians did rebel during the *fitna* period, following Muwallad rebels such as Ibn Hafsun. During the victorious campaigns that 'Abd al-Rahman III led against Muwallad rebels, the Muwallads tended to surrender, whereas in several instances the Christian rebels decided to fight till the end. Accordingly, they were executed, sometimes in great numbers, whereas Muwallads often saved their lives. In the district of Málaga, rebel fortresses which were inhabited mostly, if not exclusively, by Christians, were permanently destroyed.

Not all Christians on the rebel side were willing to sacrifice their lives. Some of the Christian notables of Bobastro, for example, are said in the Arabic sources to have favored reaching an understanding with 'Abd al-Rahman III. We would like to know more about them. Among them were two Christian leaders, 'Abd Allah ibn Asbagh ibn Nabil and Wadinas ibn 'Attaf, who, we are told, had old links with the Umayyads. Ibn Nabil travelled to Cordoba in a diplomatic mission on behalf of Ibn Hafsun and was lavishly treated by the emir. Another Christian in the same group was the bishop of Bobastro, Ja'far ibn Maqsim, who was praised for his intelligence and upright character.

But in Bobastro there was another group of Christians, headed by a man known as Rudmir, who were against any compromise with the Umayyad ruler. This group supported Ja'far ibn 'Umar ibn Hafsun as heir to his father when he died in 918. Ja'far then proclaimed himself a Christian, claiming that 'Umar ibn Hafsun had also died as one. In 920–1, Ja'far, accused of being a crypto-Muslim for showing favoritism towards the Muslims, was killed by that group of Christians. Rudmir then sent for Sulayman ibn 'Umar ibn Hafsun, who was living in Cordoba at the time. Sulayman became the new leader of Bobastro, but shortly afterwards he killed Rudmir and tortured his followers. Ibn Maqsim, who had been deposed and expelled, returned to Bobastro, but by then the leaders at Bobastro were deeply split. During the campaign of 923, the bishop was contacted by those who wanted to eliminate Sulayman, who was killed in 926–7.

These shifting alliances and loyalties show that there were sharp internal divisions within the Christians group who supported the Hafsunids from the late 910s onwards: on the one hand, the Christians who might be labelled "collabora-tionists", i.e., willing to find a place within the Cordoban polity, and on the other hand, the "rejectionists" who sought autonomous rule.

The military defeat of the Muwallad leaders and their Christian supporters went together with an increase in the rate of conversion to Islam. Although this process is difficult to gauge given the available data, the tenth century is generally believed to have been the period when Muslims formed the majority of the population of al-Andalus. In the early part of that century we still hear of Muslims abandoning a religion that had been recently adopted in their families. This was the case with Ibn Hafsun and his son Ja'far, for example, but their apos-tasy seems to have had more to do with political need to obtain the support of the "rejectionists" than with religious convic-tions. 'Abd al-Rahman III himself made political use of Ibn Hafsun's apostasy, but only after Ibn Hafsun's death, when he defeated the Hafsunids and Bobastro fell: he was then praised for putting an end to both rebellion and unbelief. But the fact is that Ibn Hafsun lived his last years as a loyal subject of the Umayyads after having abandoned Islam in the year 899, which suggests that 'Abd al-Rahman III had not had any qualms about accepting the submission of an apostate at the time. The Arabic sources do not give any indication that Ibn Hafsun repented of his apostasy between 899 and 918, the date of his death, and his son insisted that he was buried as a Christian, as we have seen, as indeed did the jurists brought along by 'Abd al-Rahman III himself when he had the Hafsunids exhumed. But the story of Ibn Hafsun's burial shows that we shall never be sure about his religious affiliation at the time of his death, for Ja'far b. Hafsun was making a bid for the support of the "rejectionists" when he presented himself and his father as Christians, and he buried his father without allowing Ibn Maqsim, Wadinas, and Ibn Nabil (the "collaborationists") to be present at the funeral. On the other hand, 'Abd al-Rahman III would have had a vested interest in presenting Ibn Hafsun in the worst possible light after the conquest of Bobastro, as this enhanced his victory and gave more religious support to his adoption of caliphal status.

Apostasy even took place within the Umayyad family. One of its members, Ibrahim ibn Ahmad ibn 'Abd al-'Aziz (a relative of the Ahmad ibn Ishaq al-Qurashi who conspired against the caliph in 936), abandoned Islam for Christianity and was executed at an unknown date. No reasons are given for his apostasy, which may have been due to the influence of a Christian relative, perhaps his mother. The information about Ibrahim is preserved in the Arabic sources because of his high social status. We shall never know to what extent his case reflects a wider phenomenon. In rebel territory, the political alliance between Muwallads and Christians (who are said to have constituted the majority of Ibn Hafsun's troops) created a context where conversion from Islam to Christianity was not punished. However, the expansion of the Muslim judicial system under 'Abd al-Rahman III must have meant that such crossing of religious boundaries from Islam to Christianity ceased to be tolerated.

Crossing them in the other direction was not only legally permitted, but also socially rewarding. Yahya ibn Ishaq was the son of a Christian Cordoban doctor who had a long career serving 'Abd al-Rahman III in different capacities such as chief of the lower police, vizier, military commander, and ambassador

to Ramiro II. But he was employed mostly as an emissary to
rebel lords and especially to Ibn Hafsun. Described as a friend
of the latter, we find him repeatedly charged with contacting
both the Hafsunids and the Christian notables of Bobastro.

An influential Christian active in the caliphal court was
Recemund, whom we have already encountered as ambassador
to Otto and the Byzantine emperor. His service to the caliph
gained him an appointment as bishop of Elvira (Granada). He is
generally considered to be identical with the Rabi' ibn Zayd
who collaborated in the production of the famous Cordoban
calendar, an almanac in which Christian lore and information
were introduced.

Among 'Abd al-Rahman III's men we also find an influential
Jew, Hasday ibn Shaprut, thanks to whom Andalusi Jewry
experienced a cultural renewal which cannot be discussed
here. He was the official representative of his community and
the caliph put him in charge of collecting the customs duties.
We have already encountered him loyally serving the caliph in
his dealings with the Christian polities: in 940 he was sent to
León to rescue al-Tujibi from his captivity; in the same year he
was in Barcelona in connection with a treaty with the counts of
the area favoring commercial exchange, and in 955 he was sent
to the court of Ordoño III. As a doctor, he cured the king of
Navarra of his obesity in 958. Hasday ibn Shaprut was involved
in the revision of the translation of Dioscorides' botanical
work, undoubtedly because of his medical expertise. That work
had arrived with a Byzantine embassy. He seems to have
learned from the members of this embassy and from traders
about the Khazars, a people in the southern Russian steppes
who had formed a kingdom and whose ruling class were
converts to Judaism; and in about 950 he established epistolary
contact with them, this time acting on his own and on behalf of
his religious community, for whom the existence of an

independent Jewish kingdom was a source of hope and pride. Ibn Hayyan describes him as outstanding among royal servants for his good mental discipline and manners, subtlety, patience, and intelligence. The names of other Jews employed by Christian rulers of the time in diplomatic activities have been preserved. This presence was surely favored by the economic role Jews played as traders. In any case, we have here an early indication of the influence Jews would have as intermediaries between Christians and Muslims in the later history of the Iberian peninsula.

6

BUILDING THE CALIPHATE: STICK, STONES, AND WORDS

Kings who want posterity to talk about their elevated aims
use the tongue of their buildings.
See how the Pyramids still stand,
whereas so many kings were erased by the ups and downs
   of time.

Verses attributed to 'Abd al-Rahman III

THE CARROT AND THE STICK

The people of Ceuta are said to have offered 'Abd al-Rahman III the government of their town because of his fame, justice, and right conduct. Many and lengthy panegyrics were written by the court poets, in which the caliph was invariably portrayed as just, generous, courageous, noble, intelligent, a gifted soldier, a thirsty sword, loving as a father, a reviver of religion, a defender of orthodoxy and a scourge of heretics, light that puts an end to obscurity, and rain that alleviates drought. The length of such poems and their praise of the caliph's alleged virtues and merits were of course usually proportional to the poets' reward. Even so, being a Sunni caliph, 'Abd al-Rahman III received more restrained eulogies than those singing the praises of the Fatimid caliphs, because the Shi'i imam was conceived as closer to prophets and saints, able to perform miracles, and having knowledge of hidden things and future events. The religious role performed by 'Abd al-Rahman III will be dealt with below. As a political leader, he appears to have mastered recourse to both the stick and the carrot.

When political expediency made it advisable, 'Abd al-Rahman III tried to win over his opponents with lavish presents, usually beautifully designed and richly textured official robes and clothes, which seem to have been highly valued by the Berber lords on the opposite side of the Straits, but which also helped persuade local rebels such as 'Umar ibn Hafsun to return to the fold of obedience. Gifts were recurrently bestowed upon his supporters. For their part, the Berber lords also sent gifts to Cordoba, consisting mostly of exotic animals, as well as horses of outstanding quality, all of which gave great pleasure to 'Abd al-Rahman III, especially because they went together with recognition of his caliphate.

We have seen how the submission of many rebel lords took two forms: either they left their former dominions to settle in Cordoba where they were enrolled in the caliphal army, or they stayed in their lands and ruled in the name of the caliph, who gave them written official recognition (*tasjil*). 'Abd al-Rahman III grudgingly conceded the possibility of sons automatically inheriting the ruling position he had granted their fathers — grudgingly because it impaired his right to choose his own representatives. The renewal of the *tasjil* for sons was a compromise solution. The caliph's ultimate aim was to put an end to the local dynasties, even as subordinates, but it was never completely achieved, as we have seen, least of all in the frontier regions.

Gift exchange mostly followed submission induced by well-calculated violence. 'Abd al-Rahman III's stick could hit hard and painfully, and it often did. Heads of Muslim rebels, of Fatimid supporters, and of infidels were sent to Cordoba from other regions of al-Andalus and from North Africa to be hung on the Bab al-Sudda, one of the gates of the Alcázar (the royal citadel), or to be paraded in the market. Defeated enemies were often executed when captured. Prisoners of war were also sent to the capital to be publicly beheaded in the esplanade between the palace and the Guadalquivir river. Sometimes punishment was intended to be especially exemplary and deterrent. This was the case with the crucifixion of the Hafsunids' corpses (in the Muslim world people were sometimes crucified alive, but more often hung up for display after execution by other means), as also with the execution in 925 of the Christian Abu Nasr, a follower of 'Umar ibn Hafsun who was famous for his skill as an archer and for having slain many Muslims. Abu Nasr was crucified alive in Cordoba, but crucifixion was not what killed him – he was shot with arrows until he died, whereupon his corpse was burnt. The tongue of Furtun ibn Muhammad, the traitor of Simancas, was cut out before he was crucified, again alive. One of the witnesses of his crucifixion fainted. 'Abd al-Rahman III is said to have resorted to the lions sent to him by his North African allies to make punishment even more terrible. They were probably never actually employed, but the mere possibility of their use was enough to generate psychological terror.

'Abd al-Rahman III accused the Fatimids of unjustly executing their servant and missionary Abu 'Abd Allah, to whom they were indebted for their success in North Africa. The Fatimids retorted that the Umayyad was incapable of differentiating between two kinds of execution: one the outcome of resentment, revenge, and tyranny, the other retaliation, just punishment, and purification. For his own panegyrists, 'Abd al-Rahman III's record of executions and deaths belonged to the latter category. But the Cordoban Ibn Hazm was critical of 'Abd al-Rahman III's recourse to violence in certain cases. He compared the caliph to his ancestor the emir al-Hakam I for his sins, his search for pleasure, and his cruelty, stating that neither had any qualms about shedding blood. Among other horrifying deeds, al-Hakam I was remembered for the massacre of the Toledan notables, for the brutal repression of the rebellion of the *rabad*, and for having ordered the castration of the young sons of Cordoban notables. Ibn Hazm's criticism of 'Abd al-Rahman III is only partially recorded. He said that the caliph ordered the sons of some blacks to be strapped to the water-wheel of one of his palaces, and used them as if they were buckets to extract water until they perished. But it was most especially 'Abd al-Rahman III's cruelty towards women and the execution of his own son that was remembered. The name of the executioner, Abu 'ImranYahya, has been preserved. He was always within the caliph's reach with his tools, which included a sword and a leather mat.

On the other hand, the caliph's panegyrists praised his just-ice and moral scruples. One day, a madman approached 'Abd al-Rahman III when he was leaving his palace and seized his horse. Managing to control the terrified animal, the caliph remained on his horse, but his guards thought that the man was a political extremist dissident trying to assassinate him, and killed him. 'Abd al-Rahman III censured them and paid com-pensation to the madman's relatives. The caliph is also described as loyal to the pacts he established with rebels and as caring for the needy in times of famine. At the same time, the memory of his attempt to usurp some pious endowments was preserved. And Ibn Hazm shockingly told how the caliph allowed his jester, a woman called Rasis, to parade with a sword and the tall headgear usually worn by scholars, in what seems to have been a mockery of both the men of the sword and of the pen. 'Abd al-Rahman III had another court jester, 'Imran ibn Abi 'Umar, who was blind.

CORDOBA AND MADINAT AL-ZAHRA'

While 'Abd al-Rahman III was busy extending his control over al-Andalus, he was also taking care of his capital, Cordoba, in several ways.

Special attention was paid to religious architecture. In 918–19, 'Abd al-Rahman III ordered the restoration of the prayer-niche (*mihrab*) of the open-air oratory, where prayers for rain and other public religious rituals were performed. 'Abd al-Rahman III also ordered the refurbishing of the courtyard of the Great Mosque and in 951 the construction of the new and monumental minaret (the Mosque tower). The facade of the mosque separating the prayer room from the courtyard was restored in 958. By then, the caliph had probably been thinking of remodelling the mosque, an endeavor carried out by his son al-Hakam II, who widened the prayer room and introduced structural and decorative changes, such as the mosaics in the *mihrab* area. The changes were meant to make the Cordoban mosque conform more closely to earlier Umayyad mosques, such as those of Medina, Jerusalem, and Damascus, all of them decorated with mosaics. These mosaics are said to have been made possible with the help of the Byzantine emperor, who supplied both craftsmen and materials, and the same is said to have been true of the mosaics in the mosque of Cordoba. We have here a conscious effort on the part of the Andalusi Umayyads to adhere to their Syrian Umayyad past, and to give artistic and religious visibility in their capital to the inheritance of their ancestors, the caliphs of Damascus. Four pages of the Qur'an owned by the caliph 'Uthman, with the blood he spilt when he was assassinated in Medina in 656, are said to have been kept in the Cordoban mosque, a relic that reminded the Cordobans of that past from which 'Abd al-Rahman III and his successors derived their legitimacy as caliphs.

The expansion of the mosque of Cordoba by al-Hakam II also was connected with the increase in the Muslim population of the town. Estimates of the population of Cordoba in the tenth century are tentative. Some consider the figure of one hundred thousand inhabitants too low a figure, but even so, if it is correct, Cordoba was the most populated European town at the time. Hroswitha, a Saxon nun writing in the tenth century, described Cordoba as "the ornament of the world."

Some building schemes, although connected with the caliph's needs, also helped to improve living standards in Cordoba. Three basins were added to a fountain outside one of the gates of the Alcázar, or royal citadel, in order to facilitate its use. The road along the river leading from the Alcázar to the palatial villa of al-Na'ura was paved in 937–8, to the satisfaction of those who had been inconvenienced by its muddy conditions during winter. Increasing fiscal revenues allowed these and other public works, such as the building of a new mint, and the rebuilding of the market, a mosque, and the post house after the fire that had destroyed them in 936. In 916, 'Abd al-Rahman III had ordered one of the gates of Cordoba, the Bab 'Amir, to be reopened, a decision that may be related with Ibn Hafsun's submission at the time and with the fact that there were now stronger military resources inside the capital. For the Cordobans, this opening of the gate surely sent the message that there was no danger of the town being attacked again. One of 'Abd al-Rahman III's first concerns was to increase the security of his own dwellings. Between the years 913–14, the gates of the Alcázar were doubled, that is, for each gate a counterpart was built, one facing the other, both guarded by porters, which resulted in more control of access to the interior. This Alcázar was the political center of the town, constituted by various palaces built by the different Umayyad rulers, and by other buildings serving different purposes in the administration. It had six gates, the most important being the Bab al-Sudda, near which the administrative bureaus were located and executions took place. Over it there was a terrace from which the caliph could contemplate the road between the Alcázar and the river. Along it, parades were celebrated and the corpses of enemies exhibited. Under 'Abd al-Rahman III, a new palace was added to those already found within the Alcázar. The cemetery where the Umayyads were buried was also located inside the royal citadel. 'Abd al-Rahman III died in 961 in Madinat al-Zahra' and his corpse was brought to Cordoba to be buried in that cemetery.

Outside Cordoba, the caliph had villas, such as that of al-Na'ura, for his enjoyment and pleasure. Military campaigns were launched from there and war captives were executed in it when the caliph was in residence. An aqueduct brought drinking water from nearby mountains to this villa. Al-Maqqari, writing in the sixteenth–seventeenth centuries, has preserved the following description:

> Water flowed through fabricated channels on a fantastic arrangement of connecting arches, emptying into a large pool at the edge of which was a lion enormous in size, unique in design, and fearful in appearance ... It was plated with gold and its eyes were two brilliantly sparkling jewels. Water entered through the rear of the lion and was spewed into the pool. It was dazzling to behold in its splendor and magnificence and its copious outpouring, and the palace's entire range of gardens were irrigated by its juices which flowed over the grounds and surrounding area.

This and other palatial villas were surpassed in beauty and magnificence by Madinat al-Zahra', on which building started around 940, after the defeat at Simancas. As we have seen, it was after this battle that the caliph stopped participating in military campaigns and concentrated instead on the building of Madinat al-Zahra', a self-sufficient city with its own mosques, baths, markets, and urban administration. Madinat al-Zahra' did not become a rival to Cordoba, however. Their mutual relationship has been best described as that of a single capital with a double pole.

Madinat al-Zahra' was built on the slope of a mountain seven kilometers west of Cordoba, where three large, stepped ter-races were cut. In the upper terrace, the residential area was situated. The middle terrace was occupied by official buildings and two wide, open gardens, one more elevated than the other. The so-called Salón (Hall) of 'Abd al-Rahman III, built between 953 and 957, overlooked the Upper Garden. It is still standing and part of his ornate decoration (to be analyzed below) has survived. A mosque was built outside the walls. Madinat al-Zahra' is said to have consumed one-third of the annual state revenues during the time of its construction. Byzantine influ-ences have been detected both in decorative motifs and in architectural elements, some of which are said to have come from Constantinople, such as an expensive enamelled basin for a fountain.

Descriptions, mostly legendary, of the magnificence, beauty, and richness of the palaces and gardens of Madinat al-Zahra' abound in the sources, especially in the later ones, often overlapping with stories told of other palaces. One of the most famous descriptions is that of the magnificent Hall with a gold and silver roof and walls of thick, coloured marble, and in the middle of which hung a colossal pearl that had been a gift to 'Abd al-Rahman III from Leo, emperor of Constantinople. The

Hall had eight doors on each side formed by marble columns that supported interlacing arches of ebony and gold, inlaid with gold, gems, and mosaic. In the centre of the Hall was a large tank of mercury:

> As the sun entered through these doors and its rays played off the roof and walls of the hall, it sparkled with light, confounding all vision. When 'Abd al-Rahman III wanted to impress visitors, he would signal to one of his slaves to cause the mercury in the tank to vibrate, whereupon there would appear in the chamber a flash like that of lightning bolts that would fill the hearts with fear.
> (translation taken from Ruggles)

Madinat al-Zahra' was the architectural counterpart of the adoption of the caliphal title. But the complex story of its construction and symbolic meaning is still only partially understood. Recent archaeological excavations are adding, and will continue to add, new data to previous knowledge.

The name Madinat al-Zahra' (the town of al-Zahra') itself is open to different interpretations. A legendary story is told according to which a slave concubine of 'Abd al-Rahman III died, leaving a large sum of money to ransom Muslim captives. But as none could be found, another concubine of the caliph, called al-Zahra', whom he loved passionately, asked him to build a town for her with that money and to give it her name. The caliph did as she asked, building a town for the recreation and residence of his slave and the notables of his kingdom. Later, the slave remarked how beautiful and white the town was, and complained of the blackness of the mountain, comparing it to a black man holding a white girl in his arms. The caliph thought of destroying the mountain, but realizing the impossibility of this decided to cut down all the trees and replace them with fig and almond trees that added the whiteness of their flowers to the whiteness of the town when they blossomed in spring.

The Umayyads of al-Andalus had previously used the root
z.h.r. (which conveys the meanings "to shine, give light, be radi-
ant, to blossom") to name some of their palaces. But the root
had acquired new shades of meaning in the context of the political and religious rivalry between Umayyads and Fatimids, and
'Abd al-Rahman III's choice of the name al-Zahra' (the resplendent one) is unlikely to have been quite so accidental as
the story of the slave girls suggests. Al-Mansur ibn Abi 'Amir
(d. 1002), the chamberlain who became the real ruler of
al-Andalus shortly before the Umayyad caliphate collapsed,
also chose the root *z.h.r.* for the town he built: he called it
al-Madina al-Zahira (the resplendent town), which clearly was
not accidental either. Al-Mansur was casting himself in the
image of 'Abd al-Rahman III. 'Abd al-Rahman in his turn was
probably trying to outdo the Fatimids.

In the official sermon that accompanied the Friday prayer in
Fatimid territory, blessings would be invoked on the Prophet
Muhammad and his family, of the Commander of the Faithful
'Ali, of his sons al-Hasan and al-Husayn, and of their mother,
the Prophet's daughter Fatima, called the Resplendent one
(*al-zahra'*). Fatima, after whom the Fatimids are called, played an
important role in their claims to legitimacy. In fact, the famous
university in Cairo, al-Azhar, which began its life as a center of
learning under the Fatimids, though it is now a bastion of
Sunnism, may owe its name to her (al-Azhar and al-Zahra' are the
masculine and feminine forms of the word). The Fatimids had
also built new towns: the fortress-like al-Mahdiyya, built shortly
after the proclamation of their caliphate, and al-Mansuriyya, a
round town imitating Baghdad, the capital built by the 'Abbasids.
Madinat al-Zahra's shape was rectangular instead.

Al-Mansuriyya was built by the Fatimid caliph al-Mansur
to celebrate his victory over the Man of the Donkey (946–7).
The Man of the Donkey was portrayed by the Fatimids as

the Antichrist (al-Dajjal) whose defeat signalled the truth and legitimacy of the victor. Now, the Man of the Donkey had sought Umayyad support and acknowledged 'Abd al-Rahman III as caliph. Consequently, his defeat, which gave the Fatimid caliph a new messianic dimension, had to be counteracted by the Umayyad caliph in order to demonstrate to his own followers that truth and salvation were on his side, not on that of his Fatimid rival. The alleged appearance of a false prophet in al-Andalus around the time of the Man of the Donkey's rebellion was intended to relocate the eschatological events in the Iberian peninsula. The remodelling of Madinat al-Zahra' around that time should also be understood in this context.

In 947, the mint was relocated from Cordoba to Madinat al-Zahra'. The decoration on the coins minted in Madinat al-Zahra' between the years 947–52 shows a proliferation of plant-like motifs. The Hall of 'Abd al-Rahman III was built between 953–7, and the decoration of its walls also shows an astonishing proliferation of floral and vegetal motifs (more than one thousand and seventy elements have been identified). A peculiarity of the Hall's decoration is that the floral and vegetal motifs, arranged alongside stems, are asymmetrical, each side being different from its mirror counterpart. As mentioned above, the Hall overlooks the so-called Upper Garden in which a pavilion, a small replica of the Hall, stands surrounded by pools. The Lower Garden lies adjacent to this garden.

This complex of Hall, pavilion, and gardens may be interpreted as a reference to Paradise, which is conceived in Islam as a heavenly lush and well-watered garden or gardens with palaces and pavilions, where male believers will have at their disposal those beautiful women, the houris. The complex could be understood as a representation of the description of Paradise in Qur'an 55: 46–78: "But, for him who fears his Lord two gardens are reserved … They have numerous

branches ... and there are therein two flowing springs ...
Therein is a pair of every fruit ... And beneath them are two
other gardens ... Of a dark green colour". The pair of every
fruit is understood by some interpreters of the Qur'an as indicating two different kinds for each type of fruit, which will
explain the asymmetry in the pairs of floral and vegetal motifs
found in the decoration of the Hall. The dark green colour of
the two "inferior" gardens would correspond to the pottery
produced in Madinat al-Zahra', which was decorated with
green and black motifs (the so-called green and manganese
pottery) over a white surface. The message that 'Abd
al-Rahman would have wanted to convey through the
paradisiac formulation of his town was that the caliph ensures
salvation and therefore it was as if Paradise already existed in
this world, in the town built by the caliph. The location of
Madinat al-Zahra' on the slope of a mountain would have
allowed believers to get a glimpse from the outside of this
earthly Paradise that reminded them of the heavenly one.

The location on the slope of the mountain has also been
interpreted as chosen to provide those inside the town with
panoramic vistas. At the same time, it represented caliphal control and dominion of the surrounding land and therefore of
al-Andalus. The gardens of Madinat al-Zahra' were also meant
to be viewed from vantage points as representations of cultivated space, thus conveying a political meaning, suggesting the
order and prosperity brought by the caliphate. If this *was* the
meaning, the contemplation of that order did not last long. By
the beginning of the eleventh century Madinat al-Zahra' had
been sacked several times in the civil wars that brought the end
of the Umayyad caliphate. The ensuing devastation and ruins
moved the poet al-Sumaysir (who died in the second half of the
eleventh century) to say: "Oh, al-Zahra'!, come back to life. /
But she answered: Can the dead return?"

THE WRITING OF HISTORY

'Abd al-Rahman III's heir to the throne, al-Hakam, was already famous for his love of books and knowledge during his father's lifetime and later, when he became caliph, he was remembered for his promotion of culture and for his commission of books. With the support of his father, al-Hakam is said to have initiated in al-Andalus the study of history and the knowledge of genealogies.

Interest in the writing of history was not limited to the ruler and his entourage. We have seen that a Byzantine ambassador had brought a copy of Orosius' history book as a gift from the emperor to 'Abd al-Rahman III. The story goes that it was translated under the auspices of the heir apparent, al-Hakam, although the identification of the translators and of the original on which the extant translation was based are hotly debated and complicated issues. For some modern scholars, the Arabic translation of Orosius which survives today looks like a work produced at the initiative of Cordoban Christians who wanted to have their own history in Arabic, the language with which they were now more familiar, for the translation includes a summary of Visigothic history which is unlikely to have been found in the Byzantine copy and would thus correspond to a copy of Orosius circulating in the Iberian peninsula. On this basis it has been concluded that there might have been two translations: one made by local Christians of a local copy, and one promoted by the caliph based on the Byzantine copy. But Muslims must be presumed also to have had an interest in the history of al-Andalus before their own arrival, and we actually know that al-Hakam was curious about Christian history, so the summary of Visigothic history might have been added to the Byzantine copy on the initiative of the caliph's son. When Hasday came back from his embassy in

Barcelona in 940, he was accompanied by Gotmar, bishop of Gerona, who gave al-Hakam a history of the Frankish kings as a gift.

Official interest was focused on Islamic history and more especially on the history of how the Umayyads had managed to achieve power in al-Andalus and to keep it. Until the tenth century, Muslim scholars had been active in spreading in al-Andalus what can be termed "Islamic salvation history," such as biographies of the Prophet and narratives about his military campaigns, stories about the pre-Islamic prophets and about pious and saintly Muslims. They had also been active in writing about the early history of the Islamic community. The establishment of the Umayyad caliphate provided the impulse for works about the conquest of the Iberian peninsula, the conquerors themselves, their internecine fights, their battles against external enemies, their genealogies (in the case of the Arabs among them), the arrival of 'Abd al-Rahman I, and the history of the dynasty he established. Since history writing was a powerful legitimizing tool, what was being recorded was, of course, pro-Umayyad history.

Ahmad al-Razi, the descendant of an Iranian immigrant who wrote historical works under 'Abd al-Rahman III, is described as the first to codify the rules of historical composition; before him, anecdotes were transmitted without much attention to their chronological framework. Ahmad al-Razi's son, 'Isa, whose history of al-Hakam II's reign has been preserved by Ibn Hayyan, said of his father that he

> collected data from old people and transmitters of reports, which he collated and organized into a history ... His work brought him close to the sovereign and earned himself and his son a greater measure of royal favour. Together they endowed the Andalusis with a science they had not hitherto practised with success.

With the two al-Razis and with 'Arib ibn Sa'id, who summarized an eastern historical work, completing it with data on the Iberian peninsula, the annalistic form of historical writing became firmly established in the Andalusi intellectual milieu.

In the history of al-Andalus attributed to Ibn al-Qutiyya (d. 977) there is not much concern for establishing a chronological succession of events. What is important is the recording of exemplary historical material serving the cause of Umayyads and, even more so, of their supporters. Ibn al-Qutiyya emphasized the deeds of certain men who had helped 'Abd al-Rahman I to become the first Umayyad emir of Cordoba or who had helped his descendants maintain their rule in al-Andalus. Those men were the past or present members of the most important *mawla* families serving in the caliphal army and administration under 'Abd al-Rahman III and his son al-Hakam II. In this way, the debt that the ruling family owed to them was highlighted, while at the same time establishing as the raison d'être of those families their engagement in the preservation of Umayyad rule. Ibn al-Qutiyya's father, who had served the Sevillan rebels, played a crucial role in their submission to 'Abd al-Rahman III, and his loyalty to the caliph from then onwards was rewarded with official appointments in the administration. His son inherited his commitment to the Umayyad cause. In Ibn al-Qutiyya's historical work, for example, the emir al-Hakam I (r. 796–822) was exonerated for the cruelty with which he suppressed the revolt of Cordoba because of the piety he showed in later life. Ibn al-Qutiyya tends to record the worthy deeds of the Umayyads, the message being that correct behavior was what allowed them to preserve their power, and that thanks to faithful courtiers and scholars they were able to govern well. Arabs were not portrayed as superior because of their ethnicity. Service to the Umayyads was what should entail privileges and rewards, and his message was that the Umayyads needed to keep this in mind.

The pro-Umayyad character of the tenth-century historical works also displays itself in the effort to make the history of al-Andalus conform to Syrian Umayyad patterns. The case of the Syrian precedent for the Byzantine origin of the mosaic decoration of the Cordoban mosque has already been mentioned (see p. 109). Al-Razi is the source quoted by later historians when they tell how the founders of the Cordoba mosque shared the church of Saint Vincent with the city's Christian population, just as had happened with the partitioning of Syrian churches between the Christian population and the Muslim conquerors, for example in Damascus, until the Umayyad caliph al-Walid (r. 705–15) purchased the church of Saint John in Damascus and ordered its demolition so that he could turn it into a mosque. 'Abd al-Rahman I supposedly did the same in 785, when he is described as having purchased the great church of Saint Vincent, demolished it, and constructed Cordoba's main Friday mosque. Many other examples can be given of the way in which the history of al-Andalus engaged in this symbolic emulation of the early history of Islam when it was written with official Umayyad support. It is because most of the sources are so obviously geared to the service of power that some modern scholars have expressed well-founded (if sometimes too radical) doubts that such historiography can reasonably be used to reconstruct the history of early al-Andalus. Apart from the Christian sources, we have no sources supplying alternative perspectives, such as those of the Arab and Berber tribal milieus or the Muwallad rebels.

SCHOLARS AND MEN OF LETTERS

While the caliph was promoting the writing of pro-Umayyad history, the religious scholars also felt the need to preserve the

memory of their own group. They did so by writing biographical dictionaries.

Compilations of biographical data on scholars involved in
the different branches of religious knowledge constitute a literary genre specific to Islamic societies, being an indispensable
element of their religious and intellectual life. An important
way in which Sunni scholars, lacking institutional background
and support, articulated their existence as a group and their
relationship to both state and society was by writing dictionaries which preserved the memory of its members, their expertise, their teachings, and their social and political practices.

The Maliki *'ulama* of Ifriqiya seem to have started writing
about themselves as a way of resisting Fatimid religious pressure and in order to preserve their Sunni tradition. Although
there are some precedents, the writing of biographical dictionaries by religious scholars in al-Andalus can be considered to
have started during the caliphate of 'Abd al-Rahman III, under
the patronage of his sons, above all the heir-apparent
al-Hakam. The Tunisian immigrant Ibn Harith al-Khushani
(d. 971) and the Cordoban Khalid ibn Sa'd (d. 963) wrote
their works for al-Hakam, while Ahmad ibn 'Abd al-Barr
(d. 949–50), who wrote about the jurists of al-Andalus, had
links with al-Hakam's brother 'Abd Allah. These biographical
dictionaries served to indicate that al-Andalus was a Sunni
society, in which religion relied upon both the scholars and the
caliph, and also to indicate that it intended to continue being
so, in contrast with Fatimid caliphal society. In fact, Fatimid
scholars were servants of the state and propagandists of the
dynasty's religion, and they wrote autobiographies recording
their services to the imams, not biographical dictionaries.

Ibn Harith al-Khushani's and his contemporaries' biographical dictionaries reflect the Maliki predominance among
Andalusi scholars, but also the changes that had taken and were

taking place in their milieu. The training of scholars favored the introduction of new trends. A crucial part of that training, especially in the early centuries when al-Andalus was still in its formative period, was travel in search of knowledge. The route followed by Andalusi scholars took them to Qayrawan, then to Cairo, Medina, and Mecca (for the pilgrimage) and, from the middle of the ninth century, also to Iraq. It was mostly through Iraqi teachers that the doctrines of the "people of *hadith*" or "Traditionists" and the jurist al-Shafi'i (d. 820) started to influence them. According to these doctrines, Muslim beliefs and practices had to be founded on both Qur'an and the model behavior (Sunna) of the Prophet, which was preserved in a series of reports (called *hadith*) recording his words and deeds. (*Hadith* is often translated as Tradition, with each individual report as "a tradition.") The first half of the tenth century saw the dedication of many Andalusi scholars, including the Umayyad Ibn al-Ahmar, to the transmission and also the writing down of compilations of *hadith*, as in the case of Qasim ibn Asbagh who in 936 dedicated his compendium (containing two thousand, four hundred and ninety Prophetic traditions) to the future al-Hakam II. But the majority of Andalusi scholars continued their dedication to Maliki law, which allowed them to earn their living as director of prayers, judges, jurists, notaries, and official witnesses. Some of them were also rewarded for legal writings commissioned by the ruler, others wrote handbooks of legal documents, much needed by the expanding judicial system.

We have already seen how the caliph sometimes required the help of religious scholars. A jurist was among the trusted men sent by 'Abd al-Rahman III at the beginning of his reign to the lords of the frontier regions in order to receive their oaths of allegiance. When 'Abd al-Rahman III visited Bobastro in 928 and ordered that the corpses of Ibn Hafsun and his sons be exhumed, the jurists who accompanied him testified that they had been buried as Christians. Jurists and Cordoban notables were sent to Toledo in 930 in order to convince its people to return to obedience, and in 937 the document of the submission of Zaragoza was signed by many jurists. Scholars of Berber origin were employed in diplomatic missions with the Berber North African allies.

The 'ulamas also performed political services for the caliph's subjects. When, in 928–9, the people of rebellious Mérida decided to surrender to the caliph, they charged their jurist, a Berber called Ibn Mundhir, to ask for peace, taking advantage of his friendship with the chamberlain Musa ibn Muhammad ibn Hudayr. Ibn Mundhir also profited from his intervention, being appointed judge of Mérida by the caliph. The history of the judges of Cordoba written by Ibn Harith al-Khushani, and his biographical dictionary of Andalusi scholars, contain many anecdotes showing the role religious scholars often played as mediators between the ruler and the ruled and among the ruled, and also many illustrating their efforts to promote egalitarianism among Muslims.

Religious scholars were not alone in their efforts to preserve their own memory. Under al-Hakam II, al-Zubaydi wrote a biographical dictionary of grammarians and Ibn Juljul one of doctors. The latter's material shows how Christian doctors, who predominated in the ninth century, were gradually replaced by Muslim doctors. Sakan ibn Ibrahim, who died in the first half of the tenth century, wrote a biographical dictionary of secretaries, the group of lettered men to which he belonged, and compilations of poetry, which abounded under the Umayyad caliphs, recorded biographical data on poets, who usually earned their living by writing official panegyrics.

Most of the poets and men of letters in Umayyad Andalus worked as secretaries of the chancery and they were not few in number: we have seen how they increased thanks to 'Abd al-Rahman III's reform of the administration (see p. 87). Secretaries required good knowledge of the Arabic language, literature, and poetry, which in its turn required "textbooks." The anthology of poetry and prose by Ibn 'Abd Rabbihi (d. 940) entitled *The unique necklace* should be understood in this context. A famous anecdote tells of how, when this work reached the east, it met with the reaction that there was nothing new in it, as Ibn 'Abd Rabbihi had limited himself to collecting eastern material for an Andalusi audience. In fact, what he was offering to his countrymen was a "vademecum" for secretaries and other men of letters, in which the latter could acquire the various competences and characteristics required of polished persons, based on eastern models developed under the 'Abbasids. The collapse of the 'Abbasid caliphate may have helped to bring eastern men of letters to al-Andalus at a time when there was a demand for them in the newly established Umayyad caliphate. The Baghdadi Abu 'Ali al-Qali (d. 967) came to al-Andalus at the invitation of the heir al-Hakam, and was lavishly welcomed and appreciated for his role in disseminating linguistic and literary material produced in the east. The reception of Eastern literary models and knowledge of pre-Islamic and classical Arabic poetry is the process often referred to as the "Orientalization" of al-Andalus. This process culminated under al-Hakam II, whose library became famous, for whom men of letters such as Abu 'Ali al-Qali, Sa'id al-Baghdadi, and the Andalusi Ibn Faraj al-Jayyani (d. 976) wrote their literary compilations. Al-Jayyani included material on Andalusi poets in his, and recorded his indignation at the contempt easterners showed for everything Andalusi.

Ibn 'Abd Rabbihi was the author of some examples of a new poetic genre, the *muwashshahat*, on which much scholarly work has been produced regarding possible and controversial influences by Romance models. But he, like his contemporaries, was first and foremost a panegyrist, the author of the long poem in praise of 'Abd al-Rahman III from which various extracts have been quoted in this book. Panegyric poetry addressed to the ruler flourished in al-Andalus under 'Abd al-Rahman III, and its authors enjoyed material privileges and social respect. Ibn Hudhayl al-Tamimi (d. 998) decided to devote himself to court poetry after seeing how many people were present at Ibn 'Abd Rabbihi's funeral.

RELIGIOUS POLICIES AND THE MALIKI IDENTITY

The Fatimid danger was military, political, and religious in equal measure, and it had to be fought not only with weapons, but also with words.

We have seen how the adoption of the caliphal title by 'Abd al-Rahman III was closely linked to his rivalry with the Fatimid caliphs, and how competing claims were reflected in the caliphal titles of the two dynasties. 'Abd al-Rahman III claimed to belong to the Prophet's family on the grounds of their common affiliation to the Northern Arab tribe of Quraysh, therefore expanding the meaning of that family against the restricted interpretation of the Fatimids, who understood it as referring to the Messenger of God's close relatives. While the Fatimids ridiculed the Andalusi Umayyads for their caliphal pretensions, reminding them that it had taken them a long time to adopt the caliphal title, the Umayyads made use of existing (and apparently well-founded) doubts regarding the Fatimid's true genealogy, claiming that they were really of Jewish ancestry. Both caliphs vaunted the great number of people who left the territory of his opponent seeking refuge in his own land.

Fatimid use of eschatological beliefs for their legitimization was paralleled by 'Abd al-Rahman III's use of the Sunni belief that the turn of a century was accompanied by the appearance of a religious renovator (*mujaddid*). The Umayyad had been proclaimed emir in the year 300 of the Muslim calendar and he stated that God had granted him the task of renewing disappearing traditions and putting an end to heretical innovations.

After the Fatimid attack on Almería in 955, 'Abd al-Rahman III ordered that the Fatimids be cursed in the Andalusi mosques. Early Muslims venerated by the Sunnis had long been cursed in the Fatimid mosques. Doctrinal and ritual differences were manifested visually and orally in Umayyad and Fatimid territories. The Fatimids added the formula "come to the best of works" to the Sunni call to prayer (Ibn Hafsun had used it during his period of obedience to the Fatimids), and abolished the formula, "prayer is better than sleep", in the call to the morning-prayer. They calculated the beginning and the end of the month of Ramadan differently, and abolished the night prayers during that month, an important ritual for Andalusis. The festival of 'Ashura' was a day of sorrow for the Shi'ites, commemorating the Prophet's grandson Husayn's death, whereas for the Sunnis it was a day of merriment and joy. When the mosque of the Fatimid town known as al-Mahdiyya was built, no minaret was erected, whereas 'Abd al-Rahman III ordered the construction of the massive minaret of the mosque in Cordoba.

Preserved material on the religious polemical exchange between 'Abd al-Rahman III and the Fatimid caliphs documents the exaggerations, deformations, and alterations to which each of them subjected the beliefs and practices of the other. The Umayyads accused the Fatimids of falsely interpreting the Qur'an thanks to their habit of allegorizing the literal meaning (*zahir*) so as to bring out its inner and occult sense (*batin*). They called them heretics who denied the prophethood of Muhammad, declared licit what was forbidden, and indulged in sexual abominations. Holy war (*jihad*) against them was better than against the Christians. The Fatimids paid back the Umayyads in kind.

An important area of disagreement was religious law. The Fatimid caliph al-Mansur issued a compilation of religious law to serve as the official Fatimid legal code; it was later superseded by a work composed by the famous Isma'ili judge al-Qadi al-Nu'man. In al-Mansur's work the caliph sets forth his rulings without referring to the pronouncements of former imams or justifying them by legal reasoning, solely relying on his own authority as the infallible imam. He unambiguously upheld the divinely sanctioned authority of the imam in religious and legal matters. By contrast, 'Abd al-Rahman III continued to play according to Sunni rules, leaving interpretation of the religious law in the hands of scholars, although, as we shall see below, his religious policy regarding Islamic law was affected by his rivalry with the Fatimids.

Among the ancient law schools, Malikism had been favored by the Umayyad rulers of al-Andalus because the other most important legal trend, Hanafism, was seen as the school of law favoured by the 'Abbasids and as having Shi'i leanings. Maliki jurisprudence contained certain interpretations (such as on arbitration) that were contrary to Shi'i doctrine. Malikism, moreover, was connected to Medina, the town where the Prophet had acted as a statesman and that had taken its name from the Prophet himself (*Madinat al-nabi*, the City of the Prophet). The reports of Muhammad's words and deeds (the *hadith*) that preserved the Prophet's Tradition mostly referred to the period when he lived and ruled in Medina. When the "people of *hadith*" and the Shafi'is criticized the Malikis for lack of conformity with the Tradition of the Prophet as collected in *hadith* compilations, the Malikis argued that they were closer to that Tradition than any other group because they were followers of Medinese legal practice, based on the imitation of what the Prophet had done and said in his town. This explains the tendency to suggest that Cordoba was a new Medina in terms of the soundness of the religious knowledge transmitted by its scholars. The mosque of Cordoba re-created the mosque of Medina and other early Umayyad mosques.

'Abd al-Rahman III continued supporting Malikism, but seems to have contemplated the idea of introducing religious pluralism in al-Andalus, as shown by the jurists he chose as judges of Cordoba. There were of course Malikis, such as Ibn Abi 'Isa, the descendant of the Berber Yahya ibn Yahya al-Laythi who was considered one of the founders of the Maliki school in al-Andalus. But there were also Shafi'is, such as Aslam ibn 'Abd al-'Aziz, a member of an important family of Umayyad clients. Another judge, Ahmad ibn Baqi (whose school affiliation is not clear), was the son of Baqi ibn Makhlad (d. 889), who had introduced into al-Andalus the science of *hadith* and aligned himself with the party of the Traditionists and the Shafi'is, suffering persecution by conservative Malikis because of it. The caliph also invited a Shafi'i scholar, 'Abd al-Salam ibn al-Samh (d. 997), to settle in Madinat al-Zahra'. Maliki scholars eventually became closer to the trends represented by the Traditionists and the Shafi'is, as can be seen in the work of Qasim ibn Asbag, the author of a compendium of *hadith* dedicated to al-Hakam when he was still heir to the throne.

'Abd al-Rahman III's most important judge was the Berber Mundhir ibn Sa'id al-Balluti (d. 966), who remained in office under the new caliph al-Hakam II. As a jurist, Mundhir belonged to the Zahiri legal school. The Zahiris were literalists or externalists who held that jurists had to follow the literal meaning of the revealed texts alone. The election of a Zahiri during the period when the Umayyad caliph was trying hard to counteract the Fatimids' victory over the Man of the Donkey is hardly a coincidence, as Zahirism represented the opposite legal doctrine to that of the Fatimids. The latter, as already mentioned, were Batinis or internalists, that is, they believed that revelation had an external form that had to be transcended in search of its occult meaning. In any case, Mundhir ibn Sa'id is said not to have judged according to his Zahiri legal school, but to have followed the Maliki legal tradition instead. The same was probably true of the other non-Maliki judges.

In fact, the appointment of non-Maliki judges was mostly a symbolic gesture indicating rejection of what the Fatimid caliphs were doing. Through them, 'Abd al-Rahman III was proclaiming his Sunnism. For Sunnis, religious scholars are those responsible of the interpretation of the revealed law, and interpretation inevitably gives rise to differences of opinion and thus to religious pluralism, best represented in the coexistence of four legal schools (Maliki, Hanafi, Shafi'i, and Hanbali), but also seen in the doctrinal diversity accepted within each school. For Isma'ilis, on the contrary, the caliph had a direct relationship with God and although he would not bring a new revelation, he was infallible in his religious knowledge of the revealed Scripture. Therefore, under his rule there was no possibility of legal or doctrinal diversity, just as there was none when the Prophet Muhammad lived. Moreover, there were no Sunni-style scholars, that is, individuals whose search for religious knowledge was born out of a personal initiative, outside the control of the ruler, and was carried out through study with different teachers (the more the better), from whom not only doctrinal contents, but also the modes of individual and social behavior were learned. Isma'ilis had missionaries or propagandists, hierarchically organized, instead of scholars; their role was to transmit the imam's teachings (or so in principle: in practice it will usually have been the missionaries who created them), and their interests lay in philosophy rather than in *hadith*.

In sum, 'Abd al-Rahman III's support of religious pluralism was another way of proclaiming that he was a Sunni caliph ruling a Sunni territory. 'Abd al-Rahman III is said in a Fatimid text to have boasted of giving his people freedom to follow the rites that they chose, claiming that because of this freedom many came to settle in al-Andalus. Religious pluralism had other advantages. When 'Abd al-Rahman III wanted to appropriate the pious endowments of some orphans, the Maliki jurists opposed him, except for one who proposed to follow the Hanafi doctrine on the matter, which would have allowed the caliph to have his way.

'Abd al-Rahman III's Sunnism was also proved by the fact that he allowed scholars to criticize him, thereby differentiating himself from the impeccable and infallible imam of the Fatimids. Mundhir ibn Sa'id, who was a brilliant preacher, censured the caliph for missing the Friday prayer during the construction of Madinat al-Zahra' and also for the materials used in building it. This criticism did not impair 'Abd al-Rahman III's status, on the contrary, it was enhanced, for only a pious, devout, and orthodox caliph would allow a scholar to upbraid him.

There were, however, limits to religious pluralism. The two half-brothers of the future al-Hakam II, 'Abd al-'Aziz and 'Abd Allah, are said to have followed the Hanafi and Shafi'i schools respectively. While the former's affiliation is open to doubt (he seems to have been labelled a Hanafi only because he was in favor of leniency regarding the drinking of wine, a doctrine attributed to the Hanafis), the latter does indeed seem to have adhered to the Shafi'i legal school. But then he was also accused of conspiring against his father, the caliph, together with others among whom there were Shafi'is, and executed around the year 950. Although the connection between 'Abd Allah's Shafi'ism and his conspiracy is not clear, his execution seems to have brought the end of Shafi'i penetration in al-Andalus. In fact, although Malikis in later times became closer to Shafi'ism, this school never managed to establish itself in al-Andalus.

Mundhir ibn Sa'id, the scholar who censured the caliph, is said to have been a Mu'tazili, i.e. a follower of a theological school that had been supported by the 'Abbasids at the beginning of the ninth century, but which was viewed with suspicion by most jurists and adherents of *hadith*. When Mundhir was identified as a Mu'tazili, it was meant as an accusation, which should perhaps be related to his Zahirism, for the founder of that school shared a fundamental doctrine with the Mu'tazilis, namely that the Qur'an was created in time (which all Sunnis denied). But Mundhir denied being a Mu'tazili, and during his judicature he was in charge of the persecution against the Masarris, who were often accused of Mu'tazilism too (among many other things). The Masarris were mystics (it was during the tenth century that mysticism became part of the Andalusi religious landscape), followers of the Cordoban Ibn Masarra (d. 931), whose doctrines could be seen as coming too close to the esoteric views of the Isma'ilis. Caliphal decrees against them were read in the mosques between the years 952 and 957. The main aim of those decrees seems to have been to put an end to religious movements and behaviors that escaped the control of the ruler and of the scholars. As Umayyad propaganda put it, "the caliph is he who stands up for Truth and brings victory for God's religion, the one who follows the path of the Rightly Guided caliphs, expels heresy and erases perdition, he is the one who dispels doubts." At the same time, in the anti-Masarri decrees, the Maliki doctrine was upheld as representing orthodoxy, emphasizing its connection with the Prophet's town, Medina.

7

'ABD AL-RAHMAN III'S LEGACY

One of the Almoravid rulers of al-Andalus at the end of the eleventh century and the beginning of the twelfth is said to have visited the ruins of Madinat al-Zahra' and criticized the expense involved in its construction. An Andalusi who accompanied him replied that the money spent on building the town had been legitimately used for that end, because it had been set aside for the ransom of Muslim captives, and none could be found during the reign of 'Abd al-Rahman III.

This anecdote reflects Andalusi criticism of the lack of Almoravid patronage of the arts, and also local pride in a past when Andalusis had their destiny in their own hands and were able to defend their frontiers without external help. 'Abd al-Rahman III's reign, in fact, soon acquired legendary dimensions and became for many the embodiment of the way things should be. When under the Party kings, taxation was denounced as illegitimate, fiscal revenues under 'Abd al-Rahman III were remembered as having been collected in accordance with the religious law.

When 'Abd al-Rahman III died on 15 October 961 at the age of seventy, the world in which he had been living was very different from that into which he had been born. The rebels who had almost brought his grandfather's reign to an end were gone, and the inhabitants of al-Andalus had become (albeit only for a short time) "a united community, obedient, quiet, subject and not sovereign, governed and not governing." Although Muslims did not expand their territory during his caliphate, frontiers were secure and within them a great impulse was given to urbanization, thus helping the penetration of military and fiscal state agents and the expansion of the world of religious scholarship.

To strengthen their rule over al-Andalus and to counteract the Fatimid danger, the Umayyads claimed their right to rule as caliphs on the basis of the inheritance of their Syrian ancestors. As caliphs, they developed an ambitious religious, intellectual, and artistic program to uphold their claim. In spite of the political rivalry and military encounters between Umayyads and Fatimids, the western Mediterranean became a space under military and political control where trade flourished. The absorption of Islamic eastern culture made the Andalusis conscious of both their superiority and sophistication compared to the Christians and their inferiority vis-à-vis the easterners. Needless to say, they responded by denying the latter. Contacts with Byzantium were of great symbolic importance in this respect, as they raised al-Andalus to the level of the great powers of the time. The minting of gold coins for the first time in al-Andalus proclaimed Umayyad economic and political power both at home and abroad.

The former ethnic and cultural heterogeneity of the population was affected by all this. A common Andalusi identity emerged both through the writing of local history from an Umayyad point of view and through the religious scholars' defence of Islamic egalitarian values. The most important feature of that identity was that it linked al-Andalus with Medina (the town where Muhammad had acted both as prophet and as statesman) through the adoption of the

Maliki legal school. Al-Andalus was on the periphery of the Islamic world, but it safeguarded the Medinese legal practice that represented orthodoxy. It was as if Medina, the town of the Prophet in the Arab peninsula, had been re-located in Cordoba, the capital of the Umayyads in the Iberian peninsula. And given that the Umayyads were the legitimate inheritors of the Messenger of God, it was as if the Prophet himself ruled over al-Andalus. Hence the pride Andalusis would always show in their unfailing orthodoxy under the umbrella of Malikism.

'Abd al-Rahman III's biographies all notice the exceptional length of his reign, unheard of at that time and even afterwards, as he ruled uninterruptedly for forty-nine years. None of his successors was blessed with such longevity. 'Abd al-Rahman III's distrust of the traditional Arab army led under his successors to an increasing reliance on Berber troops, a policy that was considered by the eleventh-century historian Ibn Hayyan as the main cause of the ruin of the Umayyad caliphate and the disappearance of the Umayyad family.

The Fatimids, whose rule in North Africa had such a great influence on 'Abd al-Rahman III's policies, moved to Egypt in 972 and gradually reduced their dependence on the Berber armies to which they owed their rise. Some years later, in 1004–5, Abu Rakwa, a man who claimed to be a descendant of 'Abd al-Rahman III, presented himself as the Mahdi and found support among Berber tribes in Fatimid territory. His defeat and execution took place in 1007; shortly afterwards, in al-Andalus Umayyad pretenders were fighting each other, contributing to the decline of the Umayyad caliphate which culminated in its abolition in 1031. For the next five centuries, no Umayyad pretender emerged to restore what had been lost. In the sixteenth century, the leader of the rebellion of the Moriscos (the Muslims who had been forced to convert to

Christianity after the conquest of Granada by the Catholic kings) claimed Umayyad ancestry to legitimize his right to rule in the Iberian peninsula. But his was a desperate and unsuccessful attempt at survival in a land where Muslims were no longer allowed to live.

Appendix

HOW DO WE KNOW
WHAT WE KNOW ABOUT
'ABD AL-RAHMAN III?

The data at our disposal about the life of 'Abd al-Rahman III come mostly from pro-Umayyad Arabic sources. The part devoted to his reign in the chronicle by Ahmad al-Razi (d. 955) is lost, but it was quoted by later historians, especially by the great eleventh-century historian Ibn Hayyan (d. 1076), whose historical compilation *al-Muqtabis* is the main source for our knowledge of the reign of 'Abd al-Rahman III. Unfortunately, only the part of the *Muqtabis* dealing with the years 912–42 has been preserved. The years 912–30 are also covered in an anonymous chronicle dependent on Ibn Hayyan. Ibn Hayyan's chronicle and other sources were used by Ibn al-Khatib (d. 1374), Ibn Khaldun (d. 1406), and by the North African historians Ibn 'Idhari (d. 1295), the anonymous author of the *Dhikr al-Andalus* (fourteenth–fifteenth centuries), and al-Maqqari (d. 1632). Ibn Hayyan's influence is also present in the parts devoted to 'Abd al-Rahman III in the histories of the Islamic world written by the eastern chroniclers Ibn al-Athir (d. 1209) and al-Dhahabi (d. 1348). The historian 'Arib ibn Sa'id (who died in the last decades of the tenth century) summarized the history of the Islamic world written by the eastern author al-Tabari (d. 923), incorporating events taking place in the western Islamic world. Only the part dealing with the years 902–32 is extant. Ibn 'Abd Rabbihi (d. 940) wrote a long poem on the first campaigns of 'Abd al-Rahman III (translated by James T. Monroe). Ibn al-Qutiyya (d. 977) did not deal with 'Abd al-Rahman III's reign in his history of al-Andalus, but his work reflects contemporary and pro-Umayyad concerns and perspectives. Ibn Hazm (d. 1064) was very critical of 'Abd al-Rahman III in his *Naqt al-'arus*.

Ibn Harith al-Khushani (d. 971) wrote a book on the judges of Cordoba in which he included those appointed by 'Abd al-Rahman III. In his biographical dictionary of Andalusi scholars, and in the later ones by Ibn al-Faradi, Ibn Bashkuwal, Qadi 'Iyad, Ibn al-Abbar, and Ibn al-Khatib, information can be found about those who lived during the first half of the tenth century. The early tenth century is also covered in the bio-graphical dictionary on doctors written by Ibn Juljul, on gram-marians by al-Zubaydi, and on scholars devoted to the "rational sciences" by Sa'id of Toledo. Views from outside can be found in the geographical work of the pro-Fatimid tenth-century author Ibn Hawqal, in the life of John of Gorze, Otto I's ambassador to Cordoba, and in Fatimid sources.

The classical work on the history of the Umayyad period in al-Andalus was written in French by Evariste Lévi-Provençal (1950–7). The articles by different authors (in English) col-lected by Salma Kh. Jayyusi in *The Legacy of Muslim Spain* (1992), and by Manuela Marín, Maribel Fierro, and Julio Samsó in *The Formation of al-Andalus* (1998) deal with different issues of the early history of al-Andalus. Both volumes include bibliographies where the interested reader will find informa-tion about the most important studies on issues such as tribal-ism, military organization, conversion, Arabicization, Ibn

Hafsun's rebellion, the Christian and Jewish population, the introduction of Malikism, and the relationship of Andalusi religious scholars with the Umayyad rulers. The situation of the Jewish community in al-Andalus has been recently discussed by David Wasserstein (1997).

Monographs devoted to 'Abd al-Rahman III, apart from those written in Arabic, have been produced in Spanish by Emilio Cabrera (ed.) (1991), Joaquín Vallvé (2003), and Julio Valdeón (2001). Eduardo Manzano (1991) has studied frontier politics under the Umayyads. Archaeological research has greatly improved our knowledge of the organization of rural and urban space. An English presentation of the archaeological findings and interpretations carried out by French and Spanish scholars is to be found in the book by Thomas F. Glick (1995). Umayyad naval policies and trade have been studied by Pierre Guichard (1979), Jorge Lirola (1993), and Remie Constable (1994). David Wasserstein has written about the fall of the Umayyad caliphate (1993).

Pedro Chalmeta (1976, 1985) has studied several aspects of 'Abd al-Rahman III's policies on the basis of Ibn Hayyan's chronicle. The studies by Miquel Barceló (1997) offer insightful analyses on Umayyad court ceremonial, legitimization, and taxation. Alberto Canto (1986) and Rafael Frochoso (1996) have studied caliphal coinage. Recent contributions on Umayyad administration and chancery are those by Mohammed Meouak (1999) and Bruna Soravia (1994). The role of eunuchs has been analysed recently by Cristina de la Puente (2003) and Meouak (2004). Diplomatic relationships are studied by 'Abd al-Rahman Hajji (1970) and David Wasserstein (1987).

The absence of Shi'ism in al-Andalus has been dealt with by Mahmud Ali Makki (1954). Contributions on the relationships between Umayyads and Fatimids have been published by Pierre

Guichard (1999), Heinz Halm (1996), María Jesús Viguera (1985), and M. Yalaoui (1973). Janina Safran (2000) has written a monograph on the adoption of the caliphal title by 'Abd al-Rahman III. The construction and meaning of Madinat al-Zahra' have been studied, among others, by Manuel Acién Almansa (1987), D. Fairchild Ruggles (2000), Maribel Fierro (2004), Félix Hernández Jiménez (1985), Christine Mazzoli-Guintard (1997), and Antonio Vallejo (1995). On art and architecture in general see Jerrilynn Dodds (1992), Félix Hernández Jiménez (1975), Nuha Khoury (1996), and the collective work *El esplendor de los omeyas cordobeses* (2001). 'Abd al-Rahman III's religious policies have been studied by Maribel Fierro (2004). Manuela Marín is the author of a monograph on the relationships between individual and society during the same time (1992). Poetry and literature have been analyzed by Emilio García Gómez (1949) and James T. Monroe (1971). A monograph on how al-Andalus adapted to eastern cultural patterns has been offered by José Ramírez del Río (2002).

The most radical criticism of tenth-century Arabic sources is by Gabriel Martínez-Gros (1992), for whom they should be taken only for what they are, the foundation texts of caliphal self-legitimization.

BIBLIOGRAPHY

Acién Almansa, Manuel. "Madinat al-Zahra' en el urbanismo musulmán", *Cuadernos de Madinat al-Zahra'* 1 (1987), 11–32

Anonymous chronicle of 'Abd al-Rahman III: *Crónica Anónima de al-Nasir*, Ed. with Spanish transl. by E.E. Lévi-Provençal and García Gómez. Madrid-Granada: CSIC, 1950

Barceló, Miquel. *El sol que salió por Occidente. Estudios sobre el estado omeya en al-Andalus.* Jaén: Universidad de Jaén, 1997

Brett, Michael. *The Rise of the Fatimids.The world of the Mediterranean and the Middle East in the tenth century CE.* Leiden: Brill, 2001.

Cabrera, Emilio (ed.). *Abdarrahman III y su época.* Córdoba: Caja Provincial de Ahorros de Córdoba, 1991

Canto, Alberto. "La reforma monetaria de Qasim", *Al-Qantara* VII (1986), 403–28

Castilla Brazales, Juan. *La Crónica de 'Arib sobre al-Andalus.* Granada: Impredisur, 1992

Chalmeta, Pedro. "Simancas y Alhandega", *Hispania* 36 (1976), 359–444

——. "La 'sumisión de Zaragoza' del 325–937", *Anuario de Historia del Derecho Español* 1976, 503–25

——. "Precisiones acerca de Ibn Hafsun", *Actas de las II Jornadas de Cultura Árabe e Islámica (1980)*, Madrid: Instituto Hispano-Arabe de Cultura, 1985, 163–75

Constable, Remie. *Trade and traders in Muslim Spain.The commercial realignment of the Iberian peninsula 900–1500.* Cambridge: Cambridge University Press, 1994

Dodds, Jerrilynn D. (ed.). *Al-Andalus: the art of Islamic Spain.* NewYork: Metropolitan Museum of Art, 1992

El esplendor de los omeyas cordobeses. La civilización musulmana de Europa Occidental. Exposición en Madinat al-Zahra, 3 de mayo a 30 de septiembre de 2001. Granada: El Legado Andalusí, 2001

Fierro, Maribel. *La heterodoxia en al-Andalus durante el periodo omeya.*
Madrid: Instituto Hispano–Arabe de Cultura, 1987
———. "La política religiosa de 'Abd al-Rahman III",
Al-Qantara XXV (2004), 119–56
———. "Madinat al-Zahra', el Paraíso y los fatimíes", *Al-Qantara*
XXV (2004)

The formation of al-Andalus. Part 1: History and Society, ed. Manuela
Marín, Aldershot: Ashgate Variorum, 1998, *Part 2: Language,
Religion, Culture and the Sciences*, ed. Maribel Fierro and Julio
Samsó, Aldershot: Ashgate Variorum, 1998, *The formation of the
Classical Islamic World*, general editor L.I. Conrad, vol. 46–7

Frochoso, Rafael. *Las monedas califales de ceca al-Andalus y Madinat
al-Zahra': 316–403H., 928–1013 J.C.* Córdoba: Junta de
Andalucía, 1996

García Gómez, Emilio. "La poesie politique sous le califat de
Cordoue", *Revue des Études Islamiques* (1949), 5–11

Glick, Thomas. *From Muslim fortress to Christian castle.* Manchester:
Manchester University Press, 1995

Guichard, Pierre. "Animation maritime et développement urbain
des côtes de l'Espagne orientale et du Languedoc au Xe siècle",
*Occident et Orient au Xe siècle. Actes du IXe Congrès de la Société
des Historiens Médiévistes de l'Enseignement Supérieur Public
(Dijon, 1978)*, Paris: Société Les Belles Lettres, 1979, 187–92
———. "Omeyyades et fatimides au Maghreb. Problématique
d'un conflit politico-idéologique (vers 929 – vers 980)". In
M. Barrucand (ed.), *L'Egypte fatimide. Son art et son histoire.* Paris:
Presses de l'Université de Paris-Sorbonne, 1999, 55–68

al-Hajji, Abd al-Rahman Ali. *Andalusian diplomatic relations with
Western Europe during the Umayyad period (A.H. 138–366 / A.D.
755–976). An historical survey.* Beirut: Dar al-irshad, 1970

Halm, Heinz. *The Empire of the Mahdi: The Rise of the Fatimids.*
Transl. M. Bonner, Leiden: Brill, 1996

Hernández Jiménez, Félix. *El alminar de 'Abd al-Rahman III en la
mezquita mayor de Córdoba. Génesis y repercusiones.* Granada:
Patronato de la Alhambra, 1975
———. *Madinat al-zahra': arquitectura y decoración.* Granada:
Patronato de la Alhambra, 1985

Ibn Harith al-Khushani. *Historia de los jueces de Córdoba*. Ed.
with Spanish transl. by J. Ribera, Madrid: Junta para Ampliación
de Estudios e Investigaciones Científicas, 1914

Ibn Hayyan. *Muqtabis*, vol. V. Ed. P. Chalmeta, F. Corriente, and M. Sobh,
Madrid: Instituto Hispano-Arabe de Cultura — Facultad de Letras,
Rabat, 1979; Spanish transl. by F. Corriente and M. J. Viguera,
Zaragoza: Anubar/Instituto Hispano-Arabe de Cultura, 1981

Jayyusi, Salma Kh. (ed.). *The Legacy of Muslim Spain*. Leiden: Brill, 1992

Khoury, Nuha N.N. "The Great Mosque of Córdoba in the tenth
century", *Muqarnas* 13 (1996), 80–98

Lévi-Provençal, Evariste. *Histoire de l'Espagne musulmane*. 3 vols., Paris:
G.P. Maisonneuve, 1950–3 (repr. Paris: Maisonneuve et Larose,
1999); transl. by E. García Gómez, *España musulmana hasta la caída del
califato de Córdoba (711–1031 de J.C.)*, in *Historia de España dirigida por
Ramón Menéndez Pidal*. Vols. V–VI, Madrid: Espasa Calpe, 1950–7

Lirola Delgado, Jorge. *El poder naval de al-Andalus en la época del
califato omeya*. Granada: Universidad de Granada/Instituto de
Estudios Almerienses, 1993

Makki, Mahmud Ali. "Al-tashayyu' fi l-Andalus", *Revista del Instituto
Egipcio de Estudios Islámicos* II (1954), 93–149

Manzano Moreno, Eduardo. *La frontera de al-Andalus en época de los
omeyas*. Madrid: CSIC, 1991

Marín, Manuela. *Individuo y sociedad en al-Andalus*. Madrid: Mapfre, 1992

Martinez-Gros, Gabriel. *L'idéologie omeyyade. La construction de la légitimité
du Califat de Cordoue (Xe–XIe siècles)*. Madrid: Casa de Velázquez, 1992

Mazzoli-Guintard, Christine. "Remarques sur le fonctionnement
d'une capitale à double polarité: Madinat al-Zahra'–Cordoue",
Al-Qantara XVIII (1997), 43–64

Meouak, Mohamed. *Pouvoir souverain, administration centrale et élites
politiques dans l'Espagne umayyade (IIe–IVe / VIIIe–Xe siècles)*.
Helsinki: Academia Scientiarum Fennica, 1999

———. *Saqaliba, eunuques et esclaves à la conquête du pouvoir. Géographie
et histoire des élites politiques "marginales" dans l'Espagne Umayyade*.
Helsinki: Academia Scientiarum Fennica, 2004

Molina, Luis (ed.). *Dhikr bilad al-Andalus*, with Spanish transl., *Una
descripción anónima de al-Andalus*. 2 vols., Madrid: CSIC, 1983

Monroe, James T. "The Historical Arjuza of Ibn 'Abd Rabbihi, a tenth-century Hispano-Arabic epic poem", *Journal of the American Oriental Society* 91/1 (1971), 67–95

Puente, Cristina de la. "Sin linaje, sin alcurnia, sin hogar: eunucos en al-Andalus en época omeya". In C. de la Puente (ed.), *Estudios Onomástico-Biográficos de al-Andalus, XIII. Identidades marginales*. Madrid: CSIC, 2003, 147–93

Ramírez del Río, José. *La orientalización de al-Andalus. Los días de los árabes en la península Ibérica*. Sevilla: Universidad de Sevilla, 2002

Ruggles, D. Fairchild. *Gardens, Landscape, and vision in the Palaces of Islamic Spain*. Penn State University Press, 2000

Safran, Janina. *The Second Umayyad Caliphate. The articulation of caliphal legitimacy in al-Andalus*. Cambridge, MA. and London: Harvard University Press, 2000

Soravia, Bruna. "Entre bureaucratie et littérature: la *kitaba* et les *kuttab* dans l'administration de l'Espagne Umayyade", *Al-Masaq* 7 (1994), 165–200

Valdeón, Julio. *Abderramán III y el califato de Córdoba*. Barcelona: Debate, 2001

Vallejo Triano, Antonio (ed.). *Madinat al-Zahra'. El Salón de 'Abd al-Rahman III*. Córdoba, 1995

Vallvé, Joaquín. *Abderramán III. Califa de España y Occidente (912–961)*. Barcelona: Ariel, 2003

Viguera, María Jesús. "Los Fatimíes de Ifriqiya en el *Kitab al-hulla* de Ibn al-Abbar de Valencia", *Sharq al-Andalus* II (1985), 29–37

Wasserstein, David. "Byzantium and al-Andalus", *Mediterranean Historical Review* 1/2 (1987), 76–101

———. *The Caliphate in the West. An Islamic Political Institution in the Iberian peninsula*. Oxford: Clarendon Press, 1993

———. "The Muslims and the Golden Age of the Jews in al-Andalus", *Israel Oriental Studies* XVII (1997), 179–96

———. "Inventing tradition and constructing identity: the genealogy of 'Umar ibn Hafsun between Christianity and Islam", *Al-Qantara* XXIII (2002), 269–98

Yalaoui, M. "Les relations entre Fatimides d'Ifriqiya et Omeyyades d'Espagne à travers le *Diwan* d'Ibn Hani", *Actas del II Coloquio Hispano-Tunecino (1972)*, Madrid: Instituto Hispano Arabe de Cultura, 1973, 13–30

INDEX